2.95

THE TV SCRIPT OF BUDDY

THE TV SCRIPT OF BUDDY

by
Nigel Hinton

edited by
RAY SPEAKMAN

Heinemann Floodlights

HEINEMANN EDUCATIONAL BOOKS LTD
22 Bedford Square, London WC1B 3HH

LONDON EDINBURGH MELBOURNE AUCKLAND
SINGAPORE KUALA LUMPUR NEW DELHI IBADAN
NAIROBI JOHANNESBURG PORTSMOUTH (NH) KINGSTON

Cover photograph by Sally Humphries shows Wayne Goddard as Buddy

First published in 1987

ISBN 0 435 23412 9

Typeset by Latimer Trend & Company Ltd, Plymouth

Printed and bound in Great Britain by
Richard Clay Ltd, Bungay, Suffolk

CONTENTS

To the teacher – an introduction

In the classroom

This version of *Buddy* offers excellent opportunities for classroom activity in the English lesson. The notes which follow, therefore, lean quite heavily towards a classroom approach. I have tried to encourage varying modes of response and avoided, where possible, repeating the pattern of the follow-up suggestions. These are addressed to the student but, of course, reply upon the teacher's judgement as to which lines of enquiry best suit a particular group. My aim has been to invite a lively response to the text and its related issues, whilst at the same time allowing for different levels of engagement with the scripts – from simple comprehension to scholarly analysis. The teacher's role in guiding, extending, supporting and discovering alternative methods of approach with the pupils is obviously central.

The suggestions are presented as follow-up to each episode. They can be used for classwork, discussion only, for private writing (in the classroom or at home), or they can be part of a 'Journal' which charts the individual pupil's response to the classroom reading. Whatever, the suggestions need sifting and selecting from, according to the level of response appropriate to the group. The last section offers some general approaches to the five episodes as a whole.

Drama

Although my reaction to the text has been as a teacher of English, I am well aware that teachers will approach these scripts for work in the Drama lesson, or for production. All of the follow-up suggestions keep this in mind and are very easily adapted for improvisation, analysis of text and consideration of technique. The text given here was adapted by Nigel Hinton from his novel for presentation as a television serial. It seems to me that an examination of the novel alongside the television script would present the student with a fascinating insight into the processes involved in shaping a television drama as well as the techniques of adaptation.

The scripts, as presented, do of course pose problems for the teacher considering this piece for production; tape/slide sequences and an open-stage production should ease these difficulties. Live music would certainly enhance a production of what is, undoubtedly, an extremely intelligent, exciting and relevant piece of drama.

Ray Speakman

BUDDY

CHARACTERS

BUDDY CLARK	13 at the beginning.
TERRY CLARK	40 – with a 'Teddy Boy' look.
CAROL CLARK	In her 30s, but looks younger.
CHARMIAN RYBEERO	In Buddy's form at school, his closest friend.
JULIUS RYBEERO	Charmian's twin brother.
MRS RYBEERO	Their mother – runs the family taxi firm from home.
MR RYBEERO	Their father.
MR NORMINGTON	Buddy's form teacher, late 40s, a traditional teacher.
RALPH CAMPBELL	'The Beast' – indeterminate age, retarded, always well wrapped up in top coat and hat which flaps over his ears.
MRS SOLOMON	Elderly occupant of the house next door to 56 Croxley Street.
DES KING	Terry's shady 'employer' – about 50 and affluent.
JOYCE	Carol's friend.
DAVID SIDDELL CLIVE TIERNON HAZEL WILSON EMMA GROVES OTHER MEMBERS OF 3E	Pupils in Buddy's class at school.
SCHOOL PREFECT	
POLICEMEN	

EPISODE ONE: RAINING IN MY HEART

SCENE 1 *A large department store.*

(BUDDY*walks through the store. He stops at a counter, picks up an item, looks furtively round, then puts it back. Moments later he is on the escalator. At the pen counter he picks up a pen, glances round and slips it into his pocket. He turns and walks away. Music: 'Holly Hop'.*)

SCENE 2 *The Clarks' kitchen.*

(*The radio is on as* BUDDY, *in school uniform, gets his breakfast. As he pours milk on to his cereal he smells burning. It is his toast. He rescues it and, although it is burnt, he slaps it on to a plate next to his cereal. He sits and turns off the radio. Just as he eats the first spoonful he hears the sound of angry voices from upstairs. He looks up, puts his hands over his ears, then switches on the radio, turning it up loud. He starts eating. Music: 'I Feel Love', Bronski Beat.*)

SCENE 3 *The Clarks' hallway.*

(BUDDY *comes out of the kitchen and stops at the bottom of the stairs. He puts down his school bag and tiptoes up the stairs. In the bedroom above he can hear the row that is going on in his parents',* CAROL *and* TERRY*'s, bedroom.*)

TERRY: Oh, Carol, leave it out.
CAROL: That's you all over, making out that I'm going on.
TERRY: You ain't, I suppose.

CAROL: No.

TERRY: Coulda fooled me.

(BUDDY *is by now outside the bedroom and is peeking in unseen.* TERRY, *wearing a T-shirt with 'Buddy Holly Lives' printed on it, is lying on the bed smoking – bleary-eyed and unshaven.* CAROL *is at the dressing table making up and brushing her hair.*)

TERRY: Give me a headache, you do.

CAROL: It's the booze gives you a headache, not me.

TERRY: I wasn't boozing. I was seeing friends.

CAROL: Yeah, your friends.

TERRY: Can't 'ave friends now, I suppose.

CAROL: You'd be better off looking for jobs instead of hanging round with that lot.

TERRY: I look for jobs. 'Ere you. I look for jobs. All right? It ain't my fault the factory closed.

CAROL: Still no reason to waste the money I earn buying drinks for that lot of . . .

TERRY: Yeah, go on – for a lot of what?

CAROL: I'm telling you straight, Terry. You get into trouble with that lot and go back to jail and that's the end. I'm not going through that again.

TERRY: That's five years ago, Carol – you don't forget nothing, you don't.

CAROL: If you'd put up with what . . .

(*She sees* BUDDY *and immediately stops and smiles.*)

CAROL: Hello, son. Haven't you gone yet?

TERRY: Wotcher, mate. Come and say hello, then.

(TERRY *pulls* BUDDY *down on to the bed, puts his arm around him and ruffles his hair.*)

BUBBY: Dad – I just combed it neat.

TERRY: Yeah – you should put some grease on it, then you could quiff it like mine.

(BUDDY *shrugs* TERRY'*s arm off.*)

BUDDY: I need four quid.

TERRY: She's the one with the money round 'ere. Ain't you, Carol?

CAROL: Don't be funny, Terry.

BUDDY: I need it. The class is going to this castle. I already had to miss the last two trips. I was the only one. You have to go in another class. It's horrible.

CAROL: I know, love, but we just can't afford it.

TERRY: We're skint.

BUDDY: Not too skint to drink and buy fags.

TERRY: 'Ere, you watch your lip.

(TERRY *aims a softish blow towards* BUDDY, *but* BUDDY *is too quick. He jumps up and knocks* TERRY*'s arm away with his fist.* TERRY *grins, trying to make it up.*)

TERRY: Come on, Buddy – don't take on.

(*But* BUDDY *is gone – out of the door.* CAROL *gives a meaningful look at* TERRY. TERRY *reaches for another cigarette.* CAROL *turns back to the mirror.*)

SCENE 4 *The Clarks' hallway.*

(BUDDY *comes down the stairs and picks up his school bag. As he does so, he glances into the living room and sees his mum's handbag lying on the sofa. He goes into the room, picks up the bag, opens it and takes out a purse. He rummages in the purse and discovers only one note – a fiver. He closes the purse, then reopens it and pockets the five-pound note. As he closes the purse he hears footsteps on the stairs. He picks up the handbag and fumbles with the catch, which will not open. He gets it open, throws the purse inside and just manages to close it and drop it back on to the sofa as his mum comes in. She looks at him strangely, then at the handbag.*)

CAROL: What are you doing?

BUDDY: Getting my things.

(*He picks up his schoolbag, shoulders it and scoots out of the room and through the front door.*)

SCENE 5 *3E's classroom.*

(*In a quiet and formal atmosphere,* MR NORMINGTON *is finishing calling the register. The pupils answer,* 'Sir'.)

MR NORMINGTON: Charmian Rybeero. Julius Rybeero. David Siddell. Anna Taylor. Clive Tiernon. Hazel Wilson. Good. Right, 3E, hands up those who brought the money for the trip to Newton Castle.

(*Everybody's hand goes up except* BUDDY'*s. He sees he is the only one, and after a slight hesitation raises his.*)

MR NORMINGTON: Excellent. I see even Clark is going to grace us with his presence this time. Very well, I'll collect the money at lunch time. And I don't need to remind you, I hope, that I expect the highest standards of dress and behaviour on the trip. There may be a laxity in such matters elsewhere in the school but I will not tolerate it in the Express Class.

(*The bell has rung during this last section.*)

MR NORMINGTON: You may go.

(*The class goes out in an orderly fashion,* BUDDY *with them. He is near the back. As he passes* MR NORMINGTON'*s desk, the strap of his old canvas bag breaks. His books scatter. He bends to pick them up.* DAVID SIDDELL *deliberately steps on one of them.*)

BUDDY: 'Ere, watch it.

(DAVID SIDDELL *passes on as* MR NORMINGTON *glares at* BUDDY'*s lapse.* BUDDY *scrambles the books together.*)

MR NORMINGTON: The Express Class is not just a question of academic excellence, Clark. I don't doubt that your promotion was justified as far as your work goes but in every other department you are sadly lacking.

(*Another book nearly slips as* BUDDY *shifts uncomfortably. He grabs it just before it falls.*)

MR NORMINGTON: Oh, go along.

(BUDDY *hurries out with the bag and books clutched clumsily to his body.*)

SCENE 6 BUDDY's *bedroom.*

(BUDDY *is sitting on his bed doing schoolwork. He is absorbed and he literally jumps when the front door slams. There are footsteps on the stairs.*)

CAROL: Buddy?

(*He gets off the bed quickly and stands up as she comes in.*)

CAROL: Where is it?
BUDDY: What?
CAROL: Don't play innocent with me. That five pounds you took from my purse.
BUDDY: I didn't.
CAROL: Don't you lie to me. It was in my purse this morning.
BUDDY: I didn't. Perhaps someone took it at your work.
CAROL: You . . .

(*She leans against the door and looks as if she might cry.* BUDDY *is shocked.*)

BUDDY: I needed it for the trip. It's all right for you. Everybody else was going.

(CAROL *begins to cry.* BUDDY *is horrified as she really breaks. He moves towards her and tries to hold her. She pushes him away.*)

CAROL: Don't you touch me. You're as bad as him. Like father, like son – that's what you are.

(BUDDY *backs away and sits on the bed.* CAROL *brushes her face roughly, then goes to the door.*)

CAROL: Thief.

(*She goes out, slamming the door.* BUDDY *slumps on the bed and cries into the pillow.*)

CAROL (*voice over*): Like father, like son.

SCENE 7 *A park (flashback).*

(TERRY *and a younger* BUDDY *are walking through a park. They stop.* TERRY *looks away, then back to the younger* BUDDY *anxiously.*)

TERRY: Now listen, Buddy. I wanna tell you something. Your mum told you I bin away working, didn't she?

(*The young* BUDDY *nods.*)

TERRY: Well, it ain't true. I've been in nick – three months for breaking and entering. But it's all over now. I've done time and that's it. We'll forget it, right?

(TERRY *looks away, then looks back really anxiously.*)

TERRY: Still love me?

(*The young* BUDDY *nods and* TERRY'*s face is transformed by smiles.* TERRY *picks* BUDDY *up and whirls him round in a hug of delight.*)

SCENE 8 *Buddy's bedroom.*

(BUDDY *grabs the pillow and pulls it over his head. Through the window we see evening turn into night.* BUDDY *is now undressed and in bed. At the sound of raised voices below,* BUDDY *stirs and wakes. He sits up bleary-eyed and listens. He almost breaks into tears as he hears the row. He lies down and covers his ears. The voices stop. A moment later his door opens. He remains turned away from the figure in the doorway.*)

CAROL: Buddy. Buddy.

(BUDDY *closes his eyes and does not move at this soft call. After a moment the door closes.*)

SCENE 9 *The Clarks' kitchen. Morning.*

(BUDDY *comes in wearing pyjamas.* TERRY, *fully clothed, is lying face down on the table, asleep.*)

BUDDY: Dad.

(TERRY *doesn't move.* BUDDY *shakes him and* TERRY *starts awake. He sees it is* BUDDY *and puts his head down again.*)

BUDDY: Dad. Where's Mum?

(*There is a long pause. Then* TERRY *sits up.*)

TERRY: She's gone.
BUDDY: *Where?*

(TERRY *shrugs and shakes his head.*)

BUDDY: Is she coming back?

(TERRY *does not reply, merely puts his head down again.*)

BUDDY: Why did she go? Dad?
CAROL (*voice over*): Like father, like son.

(*Music: 'Raining in my Heart', Buddy Holly.*)

Scene 10 *Four months later. The Clarks' house.*

(*Music: 'Raining in my Heart', Buddy Holly.* BUDDY *comes out of the front door of his house. He has changed. His hair, which was conventionally 3E–type neat, is now almost skinhead. His school blazer is very short in the arms, and he is wearing jeans and carrying a white plastic carrier bag containing his school books. He walks down the path past his dad's Harley Davidson motorbike, steps on to the pavement and begins to walk – careful of the cracks.*)

BUDDY (*voice over*): All the way to school without stepping on a crack and you can have three wishes. Mum will come home. You won't die till you're old. How old? Over fifty. You won't get in trouble for your jeans, okay. But all the way and not one crack.

SCENE 11 *Outside the school.*

(*As* BUDDY *is approaching the school – still taking care of the pavement cracks – a couple of expensive cars glide by and stop.* DAVID SIDDELL, *immaculate, gets out of one and waves goodbye to his well-heeled father as he drives away.* EMMA GROVES *gets out of the other.*)

EMMA: 'Bye, Mummy.

(EMMA's *mother says goodbye and* EMMA *joins* DAVID. *Just as they are going through the gates they spot* BUDDY. *They stop and stare.* BUDDY *sees them and stops.* DAVID *whispers something to* EMMA *and they giggle before sauntering airily into school.* BUDDY *watches them go, then, taking care with the remainder of the pavement, goes through the gate and begins to walk normally. A group of 3E pupils watch him pass, and again* DAVID *says something inaudible which causes the group to laugh.* BUDDY *tries to ignore it and walks across to the* RYBEERO *twins. The 3E group follow and saunter by provocatively.*)

CLIVE TIERNON: I bet they find it hard to walk past fruit shops.
HAZEL WILSON: Yes, all those bananas.

(JULIUS RYBEERO *turns and runs. His sister,* CHARMIAN, *calls after him.*)

CHARMIAN: Julius, no.

(*But* JULIUS *is not going for a fight. He dashes to the door, opens it and holds it open. He bows exaggeratedly to the group as if to usher them in. At the last moment he nips inside, closes the door and grins impudently. They try to push to open it.* JULIUS *holds it for a moment then dashes up the stairs as they push so that they stumble in. They charge after him and* BUDDY *and* CHARMIAN *run after them.*)

SCENE 12 *School stairway. Day.*

(BUDDY *and* CHARMIAN *are chasing the others up the stairs. As they reach the top* MR NORMINGTON *is there. He grabs* BUDDY.)

MR NORMINGTON: What do you think you're doing?

(*He clamps his hand on* BUDDY's *neck and grips uncomfortably tight.*)

MR NORMINGTON: Look at you. I told you about those jeans

yesterday. You said it was while your mother was repairing your trousers.

BUDDY: Yes, Sir.

MR NORMINGTON: Well?

BUDDY: She 'asn't, hasn't done them yet.

MR NORMINGTON: It's always you, isn't it? Letting down the standards of the rest of the class.

(*He squeezes.*)

BUDDY: Yes, Sir.

MR NORMINGTON: Yes, Sir. Well, no denim tomorrow, please, Sir.

(MR NORMINGTON *lets go and walks off down the corridor as* BUDDY *massages his neck.*)

BUDDY: Pig.

CHARMIAN: Why don't you tell him your mum's left home? He'd have to stop picking on you then.

BUDDY: My dad said I wasn't to tell anyone. You haven't told anyone?

CHARMIAN: Not even Jules.

BUDDY: Well don't. Come on.

SCENE 13 *Buddy's road.*

(BUDDY *is coming home from school. As he turns the corner he sees his dad standing next to a truck. The Harley Davidson is on the back.* TERRY *is arguing with the man inside.* TERRY *kicks the front tyre. The truck drives off.* TERRY *watches for a moment then goes inside.* BUDDY *continues towards the house.*)

SCENE 14 *The Clarks' living room.*

(BUDDY *comes in.* TERRY *is slumped full-length on the sofa.*)

BUDDY: Hello.

TERRY: Pigs. They've took me 'arley. I should've done 'im over. Only owe a couple of months. Always money, innit?

(TERRY *hits the sofa in frustration.*)

TERRY: Suppose you'll be wanting some tomorrow an' all! 'Ere, I'm talking to you.

BUDDY: I don't want any money.

TERRY: Blimey, that makes a change. Supposed to be free, schools. Don't make me laugh. If they was free, I'd still 'ave me 'arley.

BUDDY: I haven't even got proper trousers. My others are all worn out.

TERRY: Should take care of them, then.

BUDDY: I did take care of them. They're too small. I've grown. What do you expect me to do, stop growing?

TERRY: Don't you get cheeky with me. You're asking for trouble, you are.

BUDDY: Yeah, well I get in trouble for wearing jeans.

TERRY: Tough luck.

BUDDY: And it's tough luck about your Harley. It's not my fault. If you had a flipping job . . .

(TERRY *jumps up as though to go for* BUDDY. BUDDY *opens the door and dashes out, slamming it behind him.*)

SCENE 15 *Buddy's bedroom. Day.*

(BUDDY *comes in, closes the door and leans against it. He listens. His dad isn't coming. He hurls his plastic bag of books to the floor and throws himself face down on the bed. It is not the neat bed of when* CAROL *was there – just a sleeping bag. There is a call.*)

TERRY: Buddy? Do you want some tea? Buddy?

BUDDY: No.

TERRY: Come and 'ave some tea.

BUDDY: No.

(BUDDY *gets up after a moment and goes to his cupboard. From underneath a pile of clothes he fishes out a photo of his mum and dad together. They are standing outside the shop, 'Terry's Rock 'n' Roll*

Records'. They are smiling. BUDDY *puts it back under the pile of clothes.* TERRY *calls.)*

TERRY: I'm going out. Buddy?

(The front door slams and music starts from below. It is 'I'm Sorry', sung by Brenda Lee. BUDDY *runs out of his room, down the stairs and into the living room. At the window he sees his dad walking away. He turns to the record player where Brenda Lee is singing her heart out about being sorry.)*

SCENE 16 *Buddy's bedroom.*

(BUDDY, *fully clothed, is sitting up on his bed with a sleeping bag round him. He has been studying – a book is on his knee – but he has fallen asleep. There is a half-eaten piece of toast on a plate next to him. His head nods and he wakes up. He picks up the alarm clock. It is 11.20. He gets up and goes out into the corridor. He looks into his father's room and switches on the light. The bed, dirty clothes and sleeping bag apart, is empty. He switches off the light.)*

SCENE 17 *Bathroom.*

(BUDDY *is looking at himself in the mirror. He ruffles his hair then looks at his watch. He picks up the toothbrush. The tube of toothpaste is empty. He pokes the bristles into the end to try to get some paste. There's the distant sound of an ambulance siren. He listens, then begins brushing his teeth violently. He spits and is about to wipe his mouth on a towel when there is the noise of the front door. He spins round.)*

BUDDY: Dad?
TERRY: Buddy.

(BUDDY'*s face breaks into a grin of relief. He drops the towel and runs to the head of the stairs.* TERRY *is at the bottom – grinning. He holds up a brown paper bag.)*

TERRY: Get some plates.
BUDDY: What?

TERRY: Plates, cloth-ears. And knives and forks. I've got some chinky for us.

(*Music: 'It Doesn't Matter Anymore', Buddy Holly.*)

SCENE 18 *The Clarks' living room.*

(*The music continues on the record player.* TERRY *sings along with the last lines and as the song ends taps the closing 'Da da da da da' on his plate with his fork. The arm swings off the record and the machine clicks off.* TERRY *pops the last bit of food into his mouth and sits back to roll a cigarette.*)

TERRY: Ah, that's what I like – a bit of Flied Lice and Sweet and Sour Eyeballs.

(*He leans forward and ruffles* BUDDY*'s hair.*)

TERRY: What you bin doing tonight, brainbox?

BUDDY: Homework. I've got to do a speech for History about Richard the Lionheart. He got shot through the neck with an arrow and it took him days to die. He was only forty-two.

TERRY: Blimey, only a coupla years older than me.

BUDDY: I know.

TERRY: Still Buddy Holly here was only twenty-two when he died. Just think. All those great records in two years. He was fantastic. Well, I 'ad a bit of luck tonight. Met an old mate of mine. Might do a bit of work for 'im.

BUDDY: Honest? That's great. What is it?

TERRY: Oh, this and that.

BUDDY: Yeah, but what is it? Sort of factory work or what?

TERRY: It's work, all right?

(TERRY*'s snappy tone stops* BUDDY *short.*)

BUDDY: I'll wash up.

(*He begins clearing the empty plates and cartons.*)

SCENE 19 *The Clarks' kitchen. Night.*

(BUDDY *is finishing the washing-up.* TERRY *comes in and stands in the doorway.*)

TERRY: We do all right – don't we? You and me?

(BUDDY *doesn't turn round.*)

BUDDY: Course we do.
TERRY: Yeah, well . . .

(TERRY *turns to go.* BUDDY *turns to stop him.*)

BUDDY: I'm glad about the job.

(TERRY *grins.*)

BUDDY: I got all worried tonight.
TERRY: What about?
BUDDY: I don't know. Accidents and things.
TERRY: What me? You must be joking. Won't get rid of me as easy as that.
BUDDY: Do you think about it – dying and all that?
TERRY: Yeah, sometimes. Happens, don't it?
BUDDY: What do you reckon it's like?
TERRY: Dunno. Can't be much worse than this, though, can it?
BUDDY: I think about it lots. I didn't used to.
TERRY: You bin watching too many 'orror films on the telly, you 'ave. 'Ere, I 'eard a story tonight'll give you the shivers. About this 'ouse in Croxley Street.
BUDDY: Croxley Street, here?
TERRY: Yeah, Number 56. It's supposed to be 'aunted. Some geezer cut his wife's throat wiv a knife about twenty-five years ago and then went and strung 'imself up. They reckon 'er ghost walks round the rooms all dripping wiv blood. Now nobody wants to live there.
BUDDY: Don't blame them.
TERRY: Some people'd believe anything.
BUDDY: Don't you believe in ghosts?

TERRY: When you're dead, you're dead. Goodnight, mate.
BUDDY: 'Night, Dad.

(TERRY *goes.* BUDDY *picks up a knife to dry it. He looks at it, then puts it to his throat and gently draws it across. He shivers and puts the knife away into a drawer.*)

SCENE 20 *Outside a fish and chip shop. Night.*

(BUDDY, *cold, is leaning against the glass. After a moment* CHARMIAN *and* JULIUS *come out of the shop. They start walking.* CHARMIAN *unwraps the chips and hands a packet to* BUDDY. *He takes a chip.*)

BUDDY: Ta.
CHARMIAN: Not one – the bag. They're yours.
BUDDY: I never said I wanted any.
CHARMIAN: Go on. I don't want you to pay for them.

(BUDDY *storms ahead. Suddenly* CHARMIAN *rushes past and stops at a litter bin. She holds the chips over the bin.* JULIUS *runs up to* BUDDY. *They walk on.*)

SCENE 21 *Outside a cinema. Night.*

(*The three kids are looking at the pictures from a Dracula movie.* JULIUS *puts two chips in his mouth like fangs and taps* CHARMIAN *on the shoulder. She turns round and clips him jokingly round the ear.*)

JULIUS: We saw one of those on TV. Wasn't scary at all.
CHARMIAN: Some bits were.
JULIUS: It was dumb. I like monsters better than dumb ghosts and stuff.

(*They start walking.*)

BUDDY: I reckon ghosts can be scary. My dad told me about this house in Croxley Street the other day. Number 56. He said this bloke killed his wife – he cut her throat and then hung himself.

And they say her ghost walks round the house with blood dripping out of her throat and everything.

JULIUS: Here, that's great. They ought to make a film about that. Hey, let's go and look at it.

CHARMIAN: Now?

JULIUS: Yeah, it'll be better in the dark. Oh, come on, it'll be great. It's on our way home. Coming? Yeah, come on.

CHARMIAN: OK. Buddy?

BUDDY: I don't know ...

JULIUS: Yeah, come on.

(*They drag the reluctant* BUDDY *with them.*)

SCENE 22 *56 Croxley Street.*

(*The house is dark and boarded up. The three kids stand outside.*)

CHARMIAN: It's horrible.

JULIUS: Dracula's Castle, my dear.

(*He pretends to fang* CHARMIAN.)

JULIUS: Bet you wouldn't walk up to the door.

BUDDY: Dead right.

JULIUS: Chicken.

BUDDY: OK, then.

(BUDDY *goes into the garden and up towards the house. A light goes off in* MRS SOLOMON*'s house next door. We see her hand move the net curtain slightly. Slowly* BUDDY *walks up the steps to the door of Number 56. There is a noise behind him. He turns – it is the twins.*)

BUDDY: You scared me, you idiots. What're you doing?

JULIUS: Coming to look. It's only an old house.

(JULIUS *skips up the steps and bangs loudly on the knocker.*)

JULIUS: Anyone in?

(BUDDY *and* CHARMIAN *have retreated to the lawn.*)

CHARMIAN: Come on, Jules, stop being stupid.

(JULIUS *knocks again and peers through the letterbox.*)

JULIUS: There you are – nothing. Come and see.

(BUDDY *and* CHARMIAN *start to approach as* JULIUS *bends to the letterbox again. Suddenly* JULIUS *straightens up, whirls round, and dashes past them, almost knocking them over.*)

CHARMIAN: Julius, stop mucking about.

(*But* JULIUS *flies out of the gate.*)

CHARMIAN: Silly nit.

(BUDDY *and* CHARMIAN *go to the steps and peer through the letterbox. They see a flickering candle and a white face staring back at them.* CHARMIAN *screams. They spin around, jump down the steps and dash towards the gate. Music: 'Holly Hop', Buddy Holly.*)

END OF EPISODE ONE

EPISODE TWO: CRYING, WAITING, HOPING

SCENE 1 *56 Croxley Street.*

(The sequence at the end of Episode One is repeated, from the moment when JULIUS *peers through the letterbox. Following this sequence* BUDDY, CHARMIAN *and* JULIUS *are seen running down Croxley Street and through other night-time streets. Finally they race towards the twins' house, the front of which shows the sign, 'Rybeero's Taxis'.)*

SCENE 2 *Rybeero's Taxis office.*

(The three burst in through the front door. MRS RYBEERO *is at the desk giving instructions, via the radio, to one of the taxis. She signals the kids to 'Shush' and points to the other telephone which is ringing.* CHARMIAN *picks it up.)*

MRS RYBEERO (*into radio*): Anyone free to take a fare from the station? Over.

VOICE OVER (*loud speaker*): Leon here – I'll take it. Over.

MRS RYBEERO: Okay, Leon, it's a Mr Lewis. Over. Taxi on the way, Mr Lewis.

CHARMIAN: Good evening – Rybeero Taxis. Can you hold the line a moment, please.

(MRS RYBEERO *puts down one phone – picks up* CHARMIAN*'s and signals 'Coffee'. The three kids go through the office into the back room which is a living/dining room with a small kitchen off.* CHARMIAN *puts the kettle on and starts preparing a coffee.)*

JULIUS: Isn't anyone going to say anything? Blimey, we've just seen a ghost.

CHARMIAN: Ghosts don't bend down to peep through letter-boxes, Jules. And, anyway, I saw his face – it was a man.

JULIUS: Come off it. Buddy's dad said it was haunted.

BUDDY: That doesn't mean we saw the ghost. I think it was a man.

JULIUS: You said nobody lived there.

BUDDY: Maybe he doesn't live there – maybe he was just looking round.

JULIUS: Who was he then? Hey, maybe he was a murderer or a kidnapper.

CHARMIAN: Honestly, Jules, your imagination. It was probably a tramp looking for somewhere to stay the night.

JULIUS: You're just boring. It wasn't a tramp, was it, Buddy? You saw his eyes – they were loony. Weren't they?

BUDDY: I don't know.

JULIUS: Oh, blimey.

(MRS RYBEERO *comes in.*)

MRS RYBEERO: Ah swear ah going to pull them phones off the line one day. You late back. What you all been doing, eh?

CHARMIAN: Oh nothing. Is Dad out driving?

MRS RYBEERO: What you think? Him love the car more than me. Ah too plump for him now, eh, Buddy?

BUDDY: Yes. I mean no . . . I . . .

(*The* RYBEEROs *are roaring with laughter.*)

BUDDY: Honestly, I didn't mean . . .

(*The* RYBEEROs *continue to crack up as* MRS RYBEERO *pats her stomach.*)

MRS RYBEERO: Ooh, my – out of the mouths of babes and sucklings come the truth. Now see they, them phones again – they fit to drive me mad.

JULIUS: I'll go.

MRS RYBEERO: No, no – you bring a cup of coffee an' a couple of sweet biscuit. Then the two a you, straight to bed. I too plump for him, eh, Buddy?

(*She goes out, patting her stomach and flashing a smile to* BUDDY. JULIUS *goes into the kitchen and comes out with coffee and biscuits. He follows his mum into the office.*)

BUDDY: I like your mum.
CHARMIAN: Yeah, she's all right, except she makes us go to bed too early.
BUDDY: Yeah, my mum does, too.

(BUDDY *realises he is caught in a lie.* CHARMIAN *smiles, leans over and kisses his cheek.*)

CHARMIAN: Oh, Buddy.

(*She goes into the kitchen and starts tidying up.* BUDDY *follows.*)

BUDDY: Your place is nice – neat and tidy. My house used to be like this when my mum was there. Now it's just a dump.
CHARMIAN: And what do you do about it?

(JULIUS *comes in from the office.*)

JULIUS: Mum says we've got to go to bed right now.
BUDDY: I'm just going.
JULIUS: What are we going to do about the house?
BUDDY: What can we do? Anyway, it's just stupid.
JULIUS: Ah, come off it.
CHARMIAN: Buddy's right.
JULIUS: Blimey, first interesting thing that's happened in years and you . . . You're just boring.

(JULIUS *stomps out.*)

CHARMIAN: Well, I suppose I'd better go to bed.
BUDDY: Yeah, see you.

(BUDDY *walks quickly to the office.* MRS RYBEERO *is just putting the phone down as he goes through.*)

MRS RYBEERO: Goodnight, Buddy. You catching bus?
BUDDY: No, I'll walk.
MRS RYBEERO: It's cold outside. You want me call my husband? He can give you a lift.
BUDDY: No, it's okay. Does he work all night?
MRS RYBEERO: Sometime. Can't get drivers at all. So if you know any, you tell them about us. What does your father do?
BUDDY: Oh, things – you know.
MRS RYBEERO: Your mum work, too?
BUDDY: Yes. Goodnight, Mrs Rybeero.

(*He scoots out of the door.*)

SCENE 3 *Street. Night.*

(BUDDY *walks along a street, huddled against the cold. He crosses at traffic lights. As he does so, a police car arrives at the lights. The policemen look at him carefully as he turns a corner.*)

CAROL (*voice over*): Like father, like son.

(BUDDY *glances over his shoulder and sees the police car turn the corner. It cruises slowly past, and the policemen stare at him.* BUDDY *looks away. Finally the police car speeds up and goes off down the road.*)

SCENE 4 *The Clarks' house. Night.*

(BUDDY *is asleep in bed. He wakens at a noise on the stairs and sees his dad go tiptoeing by. He looks at his alarm clock. It is 3.45.*)

SCENE 5 *The Clarks' kitchen. Morning.*

(BUDDY *fills a teapot with hot water. He listens to noises upstairs that show that his dad is up and about. He tidies one or two things away including a bucket and mop. He has been cleaning and the kitchen is spick and span. He gives a last wipe to the draining board as his dad comes in.* TERRY, *still half asleep, slumps at the table.*)

BUDDY: I just made some tea.

(TERRY *barely nods his head. He takes a half-smoked cigarette from behind his ear and lights up. The ashtray is missing.* BUDDY, *who has been pouring the tea, stops and puts a clean ashtray on the table. He indicates the room.*)

BUDDY: What do you think?
TERRY: I think I want a cup of tea.
BUDDY: No, the cleaning. I've done all the rooms. Took all morning.
TERRY: You must be thirsty, then. So bring the tea.

(BUDDY *is disappointed. He finishes pouring the tea and brings it to the table.* TERRY *pours some into the saucer, blows on it and drinks. He draws on his cigarette and looks round.*)

TERRY: Make a good charlady, you would. 'Ow much do you charge? No, go on 'ow much?
BUDDY: Nothing.
TERRY: Blimey, don't never do nothing for nothing, mate. Let's see . . . I reckon it's worth . . . a tenner?

(*He takes out a wad of notes and slaps down two fivers.*)

TERRY: Go on, they're yours. Plenty more where they came from. And we'll go down the shops later – get you some trousers.
BUDDY: Where did you get . . .

(TERRY *puts his hand over* BUDDY*'s mouth.*)

TERRY: Ask no questions and I'll tell you no lies. I'm working, right? Now shut your gob and drink your tea.

SCENE 6 *Buddy's bedroom. Day.*

(BUDDY *is sitting on the bed doing up his shoes. Buddy Holly's 'Rave On' fills the house.* BUDDY *is singing along with the record when it stops and* TERRY *calls up the stairs*).

TERRY: Buddy?

BUDDY: What?

(TERRY *is at the bottom of the stairs.*)

TERRY: Make sure you got clean underpants. Don't want you showing me up in the shops. My old mum used to say 'Terry, always make sure your undies are clean. If you get knocked down I don't want the doctors thinking you run around dirty.' Poor old dear meant it, too. Bless 'er 'eart.

SCENE 7 *Streets.*

(*Music: 'La Bamba', Ritchie Valens.* BUDDY *and* TERRY *are walking down the street. As they pass a pub* TERRY *pulls* BUDDY *towards it.* BUDDY *resists but* TERRY *puts his arm round him and pulls him inside.*)

TERRY: Fancy a drink?

SCENE 8 *A pub.*

(BUDDY *sits in a corner trying to look inconspicuous.* TERRY *leaves the bar carrying a pint of beer for himself, a half pint for* BUDDY *and five packets of crisps which he drops on to the table.*)

TERRY: Didn't know which flavour, so I bought 'em all. Drink up.
BUDDY: It's beer.
TERRY: Course it is – it's a pub innit? Want one of these?

(TERRY *takes out his roll-ups and offers them to* BUDDY *who shakes his head.*)

TERRY: That's right, mate, you stay off 'em. Twenty a day at your age. Now I can't stop.

(*'Apache' by The Shadows starts playing on the jukebox.* TERRY *recognises it and responds with a quick drumming on the table.*)

TERRY: It's The Shadows.

(*He turns.* DOUGIE *is by the jukebox.*)

TERRY: 'Ere, it's Dougie. Dougie!

(DOUGIE *turns and grins a hello.*)

TERRY: Mad on The Shadows, 'e is. Always in me shop looking for their records 'e was. Do you remember the shop?

BUDDY: Course.

TERRY: The best days, they were. Broke me 'eart when it burned down. (*He brings out a clipping from wallet.*) Still got the report. Front page, it was.

(*We see the headline, 'Blaze Wrecks Disc Shop', and a photo.* TERRY *points to an indistinguishable figure in front of the burned-out shop.*)

TERRY: That's me.

BUDDY: I know.

TERRY: All them old records gone just like that. 'Course, woodentop 'ere 'adn't bothered with insurance, 'ad 'e. Was your mum mad when I told 'er.

(BUDDY *downs the rest of the beer to cover this moment.*)

TERRY: Blimey, a right little boozer. I s'pose you want another one.

(*He gets up and heads for the bar.*)

SCENE 9 *Outside the pub.*

(*The door opens.* BUDDY *and* TERRY *come out.* BUDDY *is a bit tipsy and squints at the bright daylight. He trips down the pub steps much to* TERRY's *amusement.* TERRY *takes off his dark glasses and puts them on* BUDDY. *They go off down the street laughing. 'La Bamba' is playing.*)

SCENE 10 *A clothes shop.*

(BUDDY *and* TERRY *look through a rack of trousers as a somewhat formal looking shop assistant hovers nearby.* TERRY *picks out a rather garish pair and holds them up.* BUDDY *giggles as* TERRY *holds them up against the assistant and says* 'What a wally'. TERRY *puts the trousers back and* BUDDY *picks out a pair of grey trousers.*)

TERRY: Bit boring, aren't they? What's up with a nice pair of drainpipes like these?

BUDDY: They're for school, Dad.

TERRY: Oh dear, my son's a right square. What else do you fancy? Shirts, underpants – never know. (*To shop assistant*) Might buy the whole shop, mate.

SCENE 11 *Outside the clothes shop.*

(TERRY *and* BUDDY *emerge from the shop,* BUDDY *carrying four bags in his hands. They cross the road and as* BUDDY *fumbles with the bags* TERRY *hides behind a pillar. When* BUDDY *looks up he can't see his dad. He stands bewildered a moment, then* TERRY *leaps out and scares him. They set off down the street in high spirits. 'La Bamba' is still playing.*)

SCENE 12 *McDonald's. Night.*

(BUDDY *laughs as his dad slurps the last bit of a triple milk shake. The old lady next to them, hearing the noise, turns to look.* TERRY *smiles at her and she looks away.* BUDDY *finishes his burger as* TERRY *lights up a cigarette.*)

TERRY: Bin thinking if I can get the money together I might start another record shop. That'd be a bit of all right, wouldn't it?

BUDDY: Be great.

TERRY: Get it insured this time, 'an all. Need a lot of money, though.

BUDDY: Mrs Rybeero told me they need taxi drivers.

TERRY: You're too young to drive, big boots.

BUDDY: Not me. You.

TERRY: Me, work for jungle bunnies? Do us a favour.

BUDDY: They're not jungle bunnies.

TERRY: Coulda fooled me.

BUDDY: Anyway, that's not the point. It's a good job.

TERRY: I got a job, ain't I?

BUDDY: Yeah, but . . .

TERRY: But what? I don't get you. First you moan 'cos we ain't got no money, then you moan when I make a bit. You got your trousers, didn't you?

BUDDY: I'm not moaning.

(TERRY *gets up and heads for the door.* BUDDY *fumbles with his bags and follows him out on to the street.*)

TERRY: Barrel of laughs, you are.

SCENE 13 *Outside the restaurant. Night.*

(BUDDY *comes out and joins* TERRY *who is waiting on the pavement.*)

TERRY: I'm going to work. I'll be late. Tomorrow an' all. I'll be doing nights a lot. Okay?

(BUDDY *nods.* TERRY *has been angry but now he softens.*)

TERRY: You'll be all right?

(BUDDY *nods.* TERRY *ruffles his hair and sets off down the street.* BUDDY *watches him go, then turns in the other direction.*)

SCENE 14 *Buddy's bedroom. Night.*

(BUDDY *is sitting on his bed. He is writing on an envelope, 'Savings for new Record Shop'. He takes the two five-pound notes out of his pocket and puts them in the envelope. He gets up and puts the envelope in the cupboard with the photo of his mum and dad which he looks at briefly, then closes the cupboard.*)

SCENE 15 *3E's classroom. Day.*

MR NORMINGTON: Right, off you go.

(*It is the end of registration – everyone is going out.* BUDDY *deliberately holds back – only* DAVID SIDDELL *and* EMMA GROVES *are left.* BUDDY *walks past* MR NORMINGTON*'s desk.*)

MR NORMINGTON (*pointing to* BUDDY*'s trousers*): Now, lad, that's a bit more like it.

BUDDY: Yes, Sir.

MR NORMINGTON: That bag still makes you look like a dustman, though.

(DAVID SIDDELL *and* EMMA GROVES *go past smirking.*)

MR NORMINGTON: Still, anything is better than nothing.

(*He taps* BUDDY *lightly on the side of his head with a look to dismiss him.* BUDDY *walks out into the corridor.* EMMA *and* DAVID *are along the corridor looking at a noticeboard. As* BUDDY *walks by* DAVID *sings*)

DAVID: 'My old man's a dustman
He wears a dustman's hat
He wears gorblimey trousers
And lives in a council flat.'

(BUDDY *catches* DAVID'*s shoulder and swings him round.*)

BUDDY: Just watch it, Siddell.

(DAVID *brushes his shoulder as if it were now dirty.*)

DAVID: Watch what, Clark?
EMMA: They're so violent, aren't they?
BUDDY: Just watch it, that's all.

(BUDDY *turns to go.* DAVID *sticks out a foot and trips him.* BUDDY *turns and whirls his plastic bag towards* DAVID'*s head.* DAVID *catches the bag and drives his hard case into* BUDDY'*s stomach.* BUDDY, *winded, falls back against the wall. The plastic bag splits and all the books fall out.* DAVID *and* EMMA *run along the corridor, laughing, as* BUDDY *bends to pick them up.*)

SCENE 16 *A department store.*

(*Music: 'Crying, Waiting, Hoping', Buddy Holly. An assistant is putting a red canvas bag into a paper carrier bag.* BUDDY *takes out his 'Savings for new Record Shop' envelope and pays. At the pen counter he picks up a biro, checks for cameras or someone watching – toying with the idea of pocketing it. He puts it back and walks away, pleased that he has resisted temptation.*)

SCENE 17 *The Clarks' House. Night.*

(BUDDY *comes in through the front door. 'Crying, Waiting, Hoping' is playing loudly. He puts down the paper bag and goes towards the living room.* TERRY *is sitting on the sofa looking at something. He sees* BUDDY *and quickly stuffs it behind a cushion. He gets up and comes into the hallway.*)

TERRY: Wotcher.
BUDDY: Hello.
TERRY: Fancy going to the flicks tonight? I ain't working tonight.
BUDDY: Yeah.
TERRY: Right. Have a cuppa tea first and we'll go.

(TERRY *goes off to the kitchen.* BUDDY *makes sure he has gone, then dashes into the living room and fishes behind the cushion. It is a photo of his mum.* BUDDY *looks at it a moment, then puts it back. He looks at the record player where Buddy Holly is singing, 'Crying, Waiting, Hoping', and then at the photos of Buddy Holly.*)

SCENE 18 *Outside Rybeero's Taxis office. Day.*

(BUDDY *comes along the road and is just about to reach the door when it opens and the twins rush out, calling* "Bye'. *They grab hold of* BUDDY *and pull him away.*)

BUDDY: What's up?
JULIUS: You'll never guess what. We had a phone call this morning.
CHARMIAN: Somebody rang up asking for a taxi to take them to the docks.
BUDDY: So?
CHARMIAN: So I asked them for the address where they wanted to be picked up. It was 56 Croxley Street.

(BUDDY *halts.*)

JULIUS: It's true. I heard it.
CHARMIAN: I thought I was hearing things so I asked the man to repeat it.

BUDDY: What did you do?

JULIUS: So I called the taxi, and Delgado was free so he went. Then a bit later he came back to the office and I pumped him, all casual-like.

CHARMIAN: You should have seen him – he thinks he's a real smoothie detective.

JULIUS: Get lost. I found out loads – the bloke he picked up was short, fat and he had big thick glasses and grey hair, and he was wearing a black coat. He had a suitcase and Del said it weighed a ton. He went to the docks and got out at a pub. I told you there was something weird going on.

BUDDY: It's not that weird.

JULIUS: Course it is. For a start, why's there a phone in an empty house that's all boarded up? Anyway, we'll soon find out.

BUDDY: How?

JULIUS: Cos we're going there. Now. Come on.

SCENE 19 *Outside 56 Croxley Street.*

(BUDDY, JULIUS *and* CHARMIAN *are peering round the gate at the house.*)

BUDDY: Now what? There's nothing to see.

JULIUS: How about going round the back?

(*Before anyone can stop him,* JULIUS *runs into the garden.*)

CHARMIAN: Julius! Honestly, that kid. Come on, we can't let him go alone.

(CHARMIAN *runs in.* BUDDY *watches her go, then shakes his head in worry and leans against the gatepost. He squats down.* JULIUS *dashes out and nearly falls over him.*)

JULIUS: Some bird's caught Char. I was just behind the hedge and she came belting past. Then this old lady opened the window.

BUDDY: In the house?

JULIUS: No, next door.

(*They peep round the gatepost –* CHARMIAN *is talking to someone at the side window of Number 54. She nods, runs back to the boys.*)

JULIUS: Did she tell you off?
CHARMIAN: She wants to tell me something.
JULIUS: You're not going?
CHARMIAN: She said it was important.

(CHARMIAN *walks off.*)

JULIUS: She's nuts.

(BUDDY *and* JULIUS *race after* CHARMIAN *who is already going into Number 54. They follow her up the steps. She is already ringing the bell.*)

BUDDY: What's she want?
CHARMIAN: She asked me if I like cats then she said she had something important to tell me.
JULIUS: Probably wants us to clear up some cat's mess on her floor.

(*There is a squeaking noise coming along the hallway.*)

JULIUS: Sounds as if she needs oiling.

(*They are trying to control giggles as bolts are undone and the door creaks open.* MRS SOLOMON *is sitting in her wheelchair with a cat on her lap. She gazes past them, frightened, then at them.*)

MRS SOLOMON: I saw you round here the other night, didn't I? You could get yourselves hurt, you know. I was going to warn you but I never open my door at night. Old ladies like me get mugged at night. Worse, sometimes.

(JULIUS *splutters and hides his face.*)

MRS SOLOMON: You'd laugh on the other side of your face if he caught you in his garden. It's nearly four – time for his walk.
CHARMIAN: Who?
MRS SOLOMON: The Beast, that's who. They ought to put him under lock and key before it's too late.

JULIUS: What does he do?

MRS SOLOMON: He strangles cats. He'd probably do the same for you – and good riddance. He killed my Katerina. Held up her poor little body to taunt me. I saw him from my window – I see everything from up there. He'd kill Ida too, given half a chance. But Mummy won't let him, will she, my lovely?

CHARMIAN: Strangling a cat – that's awful.

MRS SOLOMON: There, I knew you'd understand. This is Ida. Say hello to the nice young lady, Ida. And I'm Mrs Solomon – in all her glory.

CHARMIAN: How do you do. My name's Charmian, and this is my brother.

(*She stops as a dragging, shuffling sound is heard. Below them, from the side of Number 56, comes the figure of* THE BEAST. *We see only the top and back of him.* MRS SOLOMON *startles them all by shouting at him as he goes across the garden.*)

MRS SOLOMON: Murderer!

(THE BEAST *stops and stares at them.*)

MRS SOLOMON: I know all about you – don't think I don't. Comings and goings in the middle of the night. You killed my Katerina, Beast!

(THE BEAST *looks as if he might say something, but then he turns and shuffles away.*)

MRS SOLOMON: Now, don't you go hanging round there any more – especially at night. It's not safe for a young girl like you.

(JULIUS *has caught* BUDDY'*s eye.*)

JULIUS: Well, I think we'd better go now. 'Bye.

(*He and* BUDDY *race down the steps and across the garden – they peer out at* THE BEAST'*s retreating form. There is a rumble of thunder.*)

JULIUS: Come on, Cha!

(CHARMIAN *finishes talking with* MRS SOLOMON, *and runs out to meet the boys.*)

CHARMIAN: What's the hurry?
JULIUS: What do you think? We're going in there while he's out.

SCENE 20 *Back of 56 Croxley Street.*

(*The kids are looking at a small window, half-open, about seven feet off the ground. There is thunder. It is beginning to rain.*)

BUDDY: Give me a bunk-up.

(BUDDY *grabs hold of the sill and, with* JULIUS *pushing, hauls himself up.*)

CHARMIAN: Buddy – don't.
JULIUS: Oh, belt up and give us a hand.

(BUDDY *reaches the window and peers in.*)

SCENE 21 *56 Croxley Street, inside the house.*

(BUDDY *wriggles through the window into a small empty room. He jumps to the floor. As he reaches for the door handle, it begins to turn. He leaps for the window but falls to the floor as the door opens.*)

JULIUS: The side door was open.

(JULIUS *and* CHARMIAN *join* BUDDY *and the three of them go on into the main part of the house. The back room is obviously where* THE BEAST *lives. Although the light switch does not work, there is enough light from the half-boarded-up window to see the camp bed surrounded by candles and tins of food – some of them open with forks and spoons sticking in them.*)

CHARMIAN: He must eat them cold.

(*They go out into the front room. It is totally empty.*)

JULIUS: I wonder where that bloke stabbed his wife?

(*They start up the stairs –* JULIUS *first with* BUDDY *and* CHARMIAN, *who have lingered in the room, a long way behind.* JULIUS *treads on a bottle which spins down the stairs, past* BUDDY *and* CHARMIAN, *and smashes against the wall. They walk into the front bedroom which is empty except for a telephone in the middle of the floor.*)

JULIUS: Weird.

(JULIUS *leaves but* BUDDY *and* CHARMIAN *go forward and* CHARMIAN *picks up the phone. It is working. They are startled by* JULIUS*'s call.*)

JULIUS: Fancy a swim?

(*They run to join* JULIUS *who is in the bathroom. He points to the bath which is half-filled with absolutely filthy water and has foul things floating in it. They go into the hallway.*)

BUDDY: Let's just look up there and then get out quick.

(*They walk up the stairs and open the first door. An explosion of pigeons startles them. The floor is covered with muck and feathers.*)

BUDDY: Strewth.
CHARMAIN: In here?
JULIUS: Careful.

(*They close the door and enter the other attic room. There is a hook screwed into the ceiling.*)

JULIUS: Perhaps that's where the bloke hung himself.
CHARMIAN: Shut up, Jules.

(*A bright flash scares them. It is followed almost immediately by a rippling thunderclap, very near.* BUDDY *goes to the window, cleans the glass and sees the rain just starting. A figure hurries through the garden and looks up. It is* THE BEAST.)

BUDDY: God, it's him – The Beast.

END OF EPISODE TWO

EPISODE THREE: BLUE SUEDE SHOES

SCENE 1 *Inside 56 Croxley Street.*

(BUDDY *has gone to the small front window. As he cleans it, a flash of lightning lights up the sky. A figure hurries into the garden and looks up. It is* THE BEAST.)

BUDDY: God, it's him – The Beast.

(BUDDY, JULIUS *and* CHARMIAN *bolt down the attic stairs, race along the corridor and start down the stairs. There is the sound of the back door closing. They listen for a moment to the sounds that are coming from the kitchen, then* JULIUS *points to the front door indicating that to be the way out. They all agree and tiptoe down the creaking stairs, making it to the front door.* JULIUS *turns the lock. Nothing happens. Thinking it stuck, he begins to rattle it.* BUDDY *notices that there are nails at the top holding it permanently closed. There is a noise behind them. It is* THE BEAST *coming up the small flight of stairs from the kitchen area to the hallway. He is carrying a knife. The three face him with their backs to the door.*)

BEAST: What you doing?

(*They do not reply and* THE BEAST *takes a step towards them.*)

CHARMIAN: Why did you strangle the cat?
BEAST: Didn't. Didn't kill him. Found him. Put him in a hole. Lady didn't want him.

(THE BEAST'*s threatening appearance has dissolved. He suddenly notices the knife and hides it behind his back.*)

BEAST: Never killed him.

CHARMIAN: That's all right, then. We'll go and tell the lady you didn't. Would you like that?

(THE BEAST *nods, then says something inaudible.*)

CHARMIAN: Pardon?

BEAST: Mr King says no one can come in here.

CHARMIAN: We just wanted to find out about the cat. We won't come again. Okay? Okay?

(THE BEAST *nods and* CHARMIAN *begins to move forward. The boys follow her.* THE BEAST *stands in their way until the last moment, then meekly steps aside. As soon as* CHARMIAN *and* JULIUS *get to the stairs they run, open the door, and get out quickly.* BUDDY *takes his time. He looks closely at* THE BEAST *as he passes.* THE BEAST *lowers his head as if in disgrace. At the bottom of the steps* BUDDY *turns.*)

BUDDY: Don't worry. We'll tell her you didn't kill the cat.

(THE BEAST *does not register anything.* BUDDY *goes to the door, then turns again.*)

BUDDY: What's your name?

BEAST: Ralph James Campbell. 56 Croxley Street.

BUDDY: Goodbye, Mr Campbell.

(BUDDY *goes out and closes the door.*)

SCENE 2 *Outside 56 Croxley Street.*

(BUDDY *comes out of the garden and sees* JULIUS waiting outside Number 54. It is raining. BUDDY *joins* JULIUS *and they shelter under a tree.*)

BUDDY: Where's Char?

(JULIUS *indicates with his thumb.* CHARMIAN *is on the doorstep of Number 54 talking to* MRS SOLOMON.)

JULIUS: I was scared to death.

BUDDY: Me, too. Lucky she asked about the cat.
JULIUS: He's soft in the head.
BUDDY: Yeah. But he didn't kill the cat like she said.
JULIUS: She's an old witch. I still reckon there's something weird, though. Hey, I bet that Mr King's the fat bloke who called the taxi.
BUDDY: Look, Jules, you saw the house. It's just empty.
JULIUS: What about Mr King?
BUDDY: Oh, forget it.
JULIUS: Blimey, you sound as though you don't want to find anything there.
BUDDY: No, I don't.
JULIUS: Yes, you do. You keep telling me it's nothing.

(CHARMIAN *comes out of the gate.*)

JULIUS: What did she say?
CHARMIAN: Not much. I told her he didn't kill the cat. She said she might have made a mistake.
JULIUS: Nosy old busybody.
CHARMIAN: She's old and lonely, that's all. I said I'd go pop in and see her sometimes.
JULIUS: You're welcome.
CHARMIAN: What do you reckon about The Beast?
BUDDY: He's got a name. Ralph James Campbell. He told me.
JULIUS: The Beast's better. Buddy's trying to make out there's nothing going on.
BUDDY: I'm not. What did we see?
JULIUS: He came at us with a knife.
CHARMIAN: He was scared.
JULIUS: Oh blimey, not you too. Something weird's going on there. I know.
CHARMIAN: I'm going home. What about you?
BUDDY: My dad's out.
CHARMIAN: Why don't you come –
JULIUS: What about your mum?
BUDDY: Oh yeah – she's there. See you.

CHARMIAN: Buddy?
BUDDY: No, I'm going.

(*They split up.* CHARMIAN *and* JULIUS *go one way,* BUDDY *goes the other. He stops and watches them go, then heads on.*)

SCENE 3 *Dream sequence.*

(*Inside 56 Croxley Street.* BUDDY *runs into a room as* THE BEAST *come slowly up the stairs. Newspapers are on the floor, and as he looks at them a drop of blood splatters all over them. The blood also drips on to his hands. He dodges out of the room back into the corridor.* THE BEAST *is still coming.* BUDDY *dodges up the attic stairs and into the attic. There is a woman lying on the floor with newspapers around her. He bends and turns her over. It is his mum. Dead. He screams.*)

SCENE 4 *Buddy's bedroom. Night.*

(*The light flashes on.* BUDDY *is screaming.* TERRY *comes to the bed and grabs him in his arms as* BUDDY *begins to wake.*)

TERRY: Ssh! It's only a dream.

(BUDDY *wakes and clings to* TERRY. TERRY *tries to push him away but* BUDDY *clings on.*)

BUDDY: I thought you were out.
TERRY: Been back ages. Didn't half give me a turn – I was fast asleep.
BUDDY: I had a nightmare.
TERRY: You ain't kidding – must've woken half the neighbourhood. 'Ere let go of us – you're all wet. Better take that T-shirt off. Got any clean?
BUDDY: They're all dirty.
TERRY: Well, take if off anyway. We'll go down the launderette tomorrow – together, eh? Do some washing.

(BUDDY *lies down.*)

TERRY: You all right, then? (*He ruffles* BUDDY*'s hair*) You look like a brush. Skin'ead.

BUDDY: Teddy Boy.
TERRY: Proud of it, too. 'Night.
BUDDY: Leave the door open.
TERRY: Blimey, what a baby.

(*But he leaves the door open and* BUDDY *closes his eyes.*)

SCENE 5 *A launderette.*

(TERRY *has just finished loading his washing into a machine. He presses his money in and the machine starts. He then looks through the window of another machine which is working. He rotates his head with the washing, then turns to an old lady who is sitting on a bench next to* BUDDY.)

TERRY: What a pen and ink.

(*He puts a laundry basket on* BUDDY'*s head.*)

BUDDY: No! It'll get stuck.
TERRY: Oh, blimey. (*To the old lady*) Doing your smalls then, are you, saucy?

(*The old lady laughs and* BUDDY *creases up.* TERRY *hauls a couple of small cans of beer out of his pocket, and throws one to* BUDDY.)

TERRY: 'Ere are, mate.
BUDDY: Cheers.
TERRY (*to the old lady*): 'Ere, want a beer, darling? Go on, do you good.

(*The old lady smiles and* TERRY *pulls out another beer for her. He snaps it open for her and gives it to her. She drinks.* TERRY *opens his own can.*)

TERRY: 'Ere, we can 'ave a knees-up.

(*He makes a funny 'horror' face as he moves towards* BUDDY. *He sings.*)

TERRY: 'Strange things take place in my moondreams.' 'Ere, should've 'eard my boy last night. Howled the street down with a nightmare he did.

BUDDY: Dad!

TERRY: What's the matter?

SCENE 6 *A park. Day.*

(BUDDY *and* TERRY *are sitting on a park bench. The laundry bag is between them.* TERRY *is finishing rolling a cigarette.* BUDDY *is looking at a lady who is standing next to a pond with a couple of kids.*)

BUDDY: Looks like Mum, doesn't it. From behind?

(TERRY *looks and shrugs.*)

TERRY: Bit. 'Ere, I'm gonna get me 'arley back next week. Saturday. Get you an 'elmet while I'm about it. What you reckon?

BUDDY: Yeah.

TERRY: Roaring down the bypass, like I used to wiv me mates. 'Ere, might get a video now I've got a bit of cash.

BUDDY: I thought you were saving up to buy another shop.

TERRY: Well, I said maybe.

BUDDY: You'll never do it if you spend all your money on the Harley and video.

TERRY: Oh, turn it up. It's my money, right? I'll do what I want wiv it.

(*He gets up and stomps away, then comes back.*)

TERRY: Come on. Don't let's row. Fancy the flicks?

BUDDY: Aren't you working?

TERRY: No, coupla days off. Good job or you'd scream the street down again. Come on – what you fancy? 'Orror film? I know you love 'em.

(BUDDY *lunges playfully at him.* TERRY *scoots, laughing, with* BUDDY *in pursuit.*)

SCENE 7 *The Clarks' House. Night.*

(BUDDY *and* TERRY *come up the garden path.* TERRY *is carrying a packet of fish and chips.*)

TERRY: Got a key? (*He hands* BUDDY *the key*) I'll get some plates warming.

(BUDDY *opens the door.* TERRY *scoots off to the kitchen.* BUDDY *goes to close the door, then sees a figure standing in the shadows across the road. He starts, slams the door and runs into the living room. He peeps out of the window. The figure has gone. He draws the curtain quickly then peeps out of the window again. No, the street is empty.* TERRY *calls out.*)

TERRY: Come on – it's getting cold.

SCENE 8 *School corridor. Day.*

(BUDDY *is walking down the corridor with* JULIUS *and* CHARMIAN, *between lessons.*)

CHARMIAN: I saw Mrs Solomon last night.
BUDDY: Oh?
CHARMIAN: She's all right, really.
JULIUS: She's a nutter. Did she say anything about 56?
CHARMIAN: No, she just talked about cats.
JULIUS: I think we should go back for another look.
BUDDY: No.

(MR NORMINGTON *comes out of a classroom as they pass. He stops* BUDDY. *The others walk on.*)

MR NORMINGTON: Clark. I was checking the reply slips for the Consultation Evening next Friday and I noticed that I haven't had one from your parents. I trust you let them know.
BUDDY: Yes, Sir.
MR NORMINGTON: Well, are they coming? As I remember, it's usually your mother, is it not?
BUDDY: Yes, Sir, but she can't come this time.

MR NORMINGTON: Your father is coming instead, I take it?

BUDDY: I'm not sure, Sir. He might be working.

MR NORMINGTON: Is he or is he not working? I don't want to have to juggle with the times.

BUDDY: I'm sure he'll come.

MR NORMINGTON: Good. I shall want confirmation first thing tomorrow.

BUDDY: Yes, Sir.

SCENE 9 *The Clarks' living room. Night.*

TERRY: A parents' what?

BUDDY: Consultation Evening.

TERRY: You in trouble?

BUDDY: No. All the parents go. They just say how I've been getting on in all me subjects.

TERRY: What's the matter wiv reports? That's what we used to 'ave at my school. I've never 'ad to go before.

BUDDY: Mum always used to go. It's nothing, honest. We just sit there and they say what I've done in the term.

TERRY: Are you there, an' all?

BUDDY: Course I am. It's about me, isn't it?

TERRY: Sounds daft to me. What time Friday?

BUDDY: Seven-fifteen.

TERRY: Well, I might make it. But I'll 'ave to go off straight after. Give it 'ere.

(*He takes the reply slip and signs it.*)

BUDDY: Sign there.

TERRY: I know, I know.

SCENE 10 *Outside school. Day.*

(BUDDY, CHARMIAN *and* JULIUS *come out of the gates and start walking.*)

CHARMIAN: What time's your consultation tonight?

BUDDY: Seven-fifteen.
CHARMIAN: Ours is at seven-thirty. We'll see you.
JULIUS: God, I hate them. Dad always says something stupid. Last year he kept talking about ECGs instead of GCEs. Blimey, I thought I would die.

SCENE 11 *The Clarks' hallway. Night.*

(BUDDY, *neat, is standing at the bottom of the stairs. He checks his watch.*)

BUDDY: Come on. It's nearly quarter to.
TERRY: Keep your 'air on. I'm coming.

(TERRY *comes down the stairs in full Teddy Boy outfit. It's the first time we have seen him in the full regalia. He's carrying a plastic bag.*)

BUDDY: I thought you had to go straight to work after.
TERRY: I 'ave. Got me other stuff in 'ere.
BUDDY: Dad.
TERRY: What?
BUDDY: Can't you put something else on?
TERRY: It's me best.
BUDDY: I know but ... Mr Normington ... won't like it.
TERRY: He'll 'ave to lump it then, won't he?

(TERRY *goes defiantly to the door and opens it.*)

TERRY: Well?

(BUDDY *follows. The door closes.*)

SCENE 12 *A street. Night.*

(BUDDY *and* TERRY *are walking towards the school. They enter the school playground –* BUDDY *a few paces ahead of* TERRY, *who is already feeling awkward. A prefect is on the main door. He opens the door, and* BUDDY *goes through. The prefect sees* TERRY.)

PREFECT: Look at that!

(BUDDY *dies and races up the stairs.*)

TERRY: 'Ere, 'ang on.

SCENE 13 *Outside 3E's classroom.*

(BUDDY *is sitting on a chair a couple of places away from his dad, who is sitting on another one of the chairs arranged in the corridor. Some parents with a young girl walk along the corridor.* BUDDY *gets up at once to distance himself. He goes to the classroom door. The parents give* TERRY *a funny look.* TERRY *smiles ingratiatingly, then starts looking at his nails. He finds some dirt and cleans it.* BUDDY *looks through the glass in the door.* MR NORMINGTON *is interviewing* EMMA GROVES *and her parents.* BUDDY *closes his eyes in despair.*)

TERRY: Not bad 'ere, is it?

(*He plays nervously with his bag.*)

TERRY: What's this Mr Norsington like?
BUDDY: It's Normington, Dad.
TERRY: Oh. All right, is he?

(BUDDY *shrugs but, sensing his dad's discomfort, goes and sits down again – still a couple of chairs away, though.*)

TERRY: Phew, blimey. (*He's really nervous*) Never 'ad to do this before. (*He appeals to* BUDDY) I know I don't talk posh.

(BUDDY *is touched. He moves next to* TERRY.)

BUDDY: Doesn't matter.
TERRY: Well.
BUDDY: You're my dad, aren't you? That's all that matters.

(TERRY *flashes a grin of thanks. The* GROVES *family come out and go off without seeing* BUDDY *and* TERRY.)

MR NORMINGTON: Next, please.
TERRY: 'Ere goes.

(*He wipes his hands nervously on his jacket and they go in.* MR NORMINGTON *stands up. His smile freezes, then unfreezes with difficulty.*)

MR NORMINGTON: Ah, Mr Clark. How do you do?

(TERRY *holds out his plastic bag. Laughs, then dumps it on the desk and grabs* MR NORMINGTON'*s hand – evidently too firmly.*)

TERRY: Pleased to meet you, I'm sure.

MR NORMINGTON: Yes, well . . . Do sit down Mr Clark, and you, Buddy. Right, where shall we begin? The reports first, perhaps.

(*The plastic bag is on the reports.* BUDDY *quickly grabs it.*)

MR NORMINGTON: Well, this shouldn't take very long – they're all very good, I'm pleased to say.

TERRY: Oh – nice.

MR NORMINGTON: Maths – 'Excellent work'. English – 'Very good work. Shows imaginative flair'.

TERRY: Oh – nice.

(MR NORMINGTON *rattles through the rest.*)

MR NORMINGTON: History – 'Consistently good essays'. Geography – 'Fair'. Physics – 'Works well'. Biology – 'Good work'. Sociology – 'Good'. Computer Studies – 'Good grasp of basics'. Art – 'Not particularly talented but tries hard'. French – 'Good accent. Good grasp of grammar'. Well, not much to complain about there, is there? As you can see from these comments, Mr Clark, Buddy is doing very well in 3E. We're very pleased with him.

TERRY: Right brain-box, in't 'e?

MR NORMINGTON: Yes. Well, I know it's a long way off yet, but we're expecting very good things from him in the public examinations.

TERRY: Oh – nice.

MR NORMINGTON: Have you talked about careers yet?

(TERRY *is stumped.*)

BUDDY: Well, we've talked about some things but I haven't made up my mind yet.

MR NORMINGTON: Early days. I'm sorry, Mr Clark, I can't recall what you do for a living. (*Checks record card*) Oh yes – you work for Bradley's. Didn't they close the factory down?

TERRY: Yeah, last year. Want one of these?

(*He offers* MR NORMINGTON *a roll-up*)

MR NORMINGTON: No, thank you.

TERRY: I do a bit wiv antiques on the side, now. I'm 'oping to 'ave a shop like what I used to 'ave.

MR NORMINGTON: Fine. Well, I don't think there's much else from our end. Unless, of course, you've got any problems at your end?

TERRY: No, everyfink's fine.

MR NORMINGTON: Good. How's Mrs Clark? Well, I trust.

TERRY: Oh yeah – she's okay.

MR NORMINGTON: Good. Give her my regards.

TERRY: Yeah, I will.

MR NORMINGTON: Good. Well, thank you for coming, Mr Clark.

TERRY: Yeah. Nice to meet you. Goodnight. Thank you very much.

(BUDDY *and* TERRY *walk out of the door.* BUDDY *closes it. The* RYBEERO *twins are outside with their parents.*)

CHARMIAN: How was it?

BUDDY: Okay. This is Charmian and Julius, my friends. And this is Mr and Mrs Rybeero. My dad.

MR RYBEERO: How do you do?

MRS RYBEERO: Hello.

TERRY: Nice to meet you.

MRS RYBEERO: My, you dress up real nice, Mr Clark. It bring back the good old days. Rock 'n' Roll.

TERRY: Oh, you like Rock 'n' Roll, then?

MR RYBEERO: Sure do. Fats Domino. Clyde MacPhatter.

MRS RYBEERO: Little Richard. I play him all the time.

TERRY: Yeah, them black singers was great. Buddy Holly was the King, though. I saw 'im, you know – in '58 when 'e was over 'ere. Cor, 'e was brilliant. There was somefing about 'im – 'is voice an' all. It was like 'e was singing fings you knew about. Fings that 'ad 'appened to you. Know what I mean?

MRS RYBEERO: Ah certainly do.

(*There is a cough from the doorway.* MR NORMINGTON *is waiting. He smiles falsely and the* RYBEEROs *go in.* JULIUS *and* CHARMIAN *follow.*)

TERRY: Good luck.

JULIUS: Blimey, great start.

(BUDDY *and* TERRY *walk along the corridor.*)

BUDDY: It's this way, Dad.

TERRY: Fancy them liking Rock 'n' Roll. They're all right, ain't they. That Normington bloke's a bit of a berk, though, ain't 'e.

SCENE 14 *Street. Night.*

(BUDDY *and* TERRY *are walking. They come to a junction.*)

TERRY: Right then. I'm off. You be okay going 'ome? And no screaming the street down, right?

(*He ruffles* BUDDY'*s hair and they go on their separate ways.*)

SCENE 15 *The Clarks' house.*

(BUDDY *comes up the garden path, opens the door and goes in. As he closes the door, he sees a figure in the shadows across the street. He slams the door, runs into the kitchen and grabs a knife from the drawer. He runs upstairs as there is a loud ring on the bell.*)

BUDDY: The Beast!

(BUDDY *comes down the stairs and sees, through the door glass, a figure step back. He fumbles with the door and opens it. It is* CAROL CLARK. *Her hair is cut differently.*)

CAROL: Hello, Buddy.
BUDDY: Hello.

(*He holds the door open wide so she can come in but she shakes her head.* BUDDY *feels awkward and clumsy. He plays with the latch.*)

CAROL: You don't seem very pleased to see me.

(BUDDY *continues to flick the catch.*)

CAROL: I'd better go, then.

(BUDDY *hides his face behind the door.*)

CAROL: You all right?

(BUDDY *nods but is struggling not to cry.*)

CAROL: Why are you all in the dark?
BUDDY: I thought you were someone else.
CAROL: You're not in trouble, are you? Sure? I'd better go.

(*She starts down the path.* BUDDY *closes the door, then slumps on to the bottom of the stairs, crying. The bell rings again.* BUDDY *roughly wipes away the tears and opens the door.*)

CAROL: Buddy, I don't want to stay here in case your dad comes. Come out for a walk with me. Please.

SCENE 16 *A bus station café.*

(BUDDY *is sitting at a table.* CAROL *comes back from the counter with a coke, tea and a doughnut. She sits down.*)

CAROL: You haven't half grown. Nearly taller than me.

(BUDDY *picks up the salt. He pours some on the table and plays with it with his finger. He makes an 'O' on the table, without looking up.*)

BUDDY: I'm sorry.
CAROL: What?
BUDDY: About that money.

CAROL: What money?

BUDDY: I thought ...

CAROL: What, my love? Tell me.

BUDDY: I thought you went away because I stole the money from your purse.

(CAROL *puts her hand to her mouth and closes her eyes. She shakes her head. She is in such evident distress that* BUDDY *glances round, then takes her free hand in his. She grips it.*)

CAROL: It's not true. Don't ever think it. Never. Promise me.

BUDDY: I promise.

(CAROL *lets go of his hand.*)

CAROL: I had to get away. Not because of you. Not even because of your dad. It was for me. I can't explain. I still love you. Both of you.

BUDDY: Will you come home?

CAROL: I can't – not just like that.

(*She begins turning her cup in the saucer – at a loss.*)

BUDDY: Do you love someone else?

CAROL: No. No. Lots of times I nearly came back. Last Sunday I went round the house. I saw you with your dad and all I wanted to do was come in and see you both – talk to you. But I knew it wouldn't be any good. It would all be the same, like before. The rows. I got married too young. Had you too young. I missed out on everything. I'm not a very good mum.

BUDDY: You are. Don't say that. You are.

CAROL: Here, I'm going to school now – evening classes. Business Studies – three evenings a week. I'm a right dunce.

BUDDY: I bet you're not.

CAROL: If I pass the exams I'm going to get a better job. Is your dad working?

BUDDY: He might get a job driving taxis. They need drivers.

(CAROL *tries a smile but can't.*)

SCENE 17 *Streets. Night.*

(CAROL *and* BUDDY *are walking.*)

CAROL: I've got a lovely flat. I share it with Joyce – one of the girls from the office. She's been ever so nice to me.

(*They walk a bit further.* CAROL *stops and fumbles with her bag.*)

CAROL: I won't come all the way back. I've written down the address. You can come and see me – any time. Buddy, you mustn't hate me for what I've done.

BUDDY: I don't. I love you.

CAROL: Here's some money. No, please take it. Buddy, please.

(*He takes the money and the address.*)

BUDDY: Dad loves you. He's going to save up and buy a shop again. He looks at your photo. Honest. I know he loves you. He wants you to come back home. So do I.

CAROL: I can't. Not yet. Come and see me. Don't say anything to your dad. Just give me time. Buddy?

(*He nods.* CAROL *walks away, turns and waves.* BUDDY *waves, then begins walking. A grin of delight breaks on his face. He begins to run.*)

END OF EPISODE THREE

EPISODE FOUR: THAT'LL BE THE DAY

SCENE 1 *Outside a motorbike shop.*

(BUDDY *and* TERRY *come out of the shop carrying helmets. The shopkeeper is with them as they walk across the forecourt to where the Harley Davidson is waiting.* TERRY *strokes it like an old friend, while* BUDDY *puts his helmet on.* TERRY *follows suit.*)

TERRY: 'We've looked after it nicely for you, Mr Clark. We all run short sometimes, Mr Clark.' (*He calls back to the shopkeeper*) You know what? You're a prat!

(*The shopkeeper walks off.* TERRY *and* BUDDY *sit astride the bike.*)

TERRY: See what a bit of money can do? Let's burn some road.

(*Music: 'Rip It Up', Elvis Presley. The bike roars into life. As the music plays we see* TERRY *burning up cars, taking corners at speed and screaming down a dual-carriageway. He bumps off the road and seems to be heading for a cliff edge. At the last moment he skids away and stops. The music ends abruptly as* BUDDY *leaps from the saddle.*)

BUDDY: You're mad. We could've gone over the edge.
TERRY: Chick, chick, chicken.
BUDDY: I don't care. You're stupid.
TERRY: Nah, it's great. Gotta take a few risks.
BUDDY: Yeah, it's all right for you.

(*He lashes out at* TERRY*'s arm.*)

TERRY: 'Ere, do that again and I'll knock your block off.

(BUDDY *races away over the grass and down the road. The bike roars past.* TERRY *stops.* BUDDY *walks past.* TERRY *cruises alongside.*)

TERRY: Okay, I'm sorry. (*He taps* BUDDY*'s helmet*) My nut's as thick as this. Come on – get on.

(*He grins and* BUDDY *relents.* BUDDY *climbs on to the bike. Music: 'Rip It Up'.*)

SCENE 2 *A seaside café.*

(TERRY *is playing a pinball machine.* BUDDY *is watching in admiration.* TERRY *flips away and the ball finally eludes him. 'That'll Be the Day' plays on the jukebox.*)

BUDDY: Blimey, you're really good.

TERRY: Course I am. All them years down Rube's caff when I should've been in school. Mind, I'd rather be a genius like you – I ain't kidding, neither. Now look what you've made me do. Oh well, gotta go to work.

BUDDY: Do you have to?

TERRY: Don't start. (TERRY *picks up his helmet and walks to the door*) Come on.

SCENE 3 *Outside the Clarks' house. Night.*

(*The bike cruises smoothly to the gate.* BUDDY *gets off.* TERRY *raps* BUDDY*'s helmet in farewell.*)

BUDDY: Dad . . .

TERRY: See you later.

(*But* TERRY *revs up and is gone.* BUDDY *wanders up the path to the door.*)

SCENE 4 *Buddy's bedroom. Night.*

(BUDDY *is in bed asleep.*)

TERRY: Buddy! Buddy!

(BUDDY *starts awake.*)

BUDDY: Dad?

(*He gets up quickly and goes into the corridor.*)

BUDDY: Dad?
TERRY: In here.

(*'Here' is the bathroom.* BUDDY *moves to the door. He reaches for the handle. There is blood running down the paintwork and drops of blood all over the lino.*)

TERRY: No, don't come in. Stay there.
BUDDY: Dad!
TERRY: Now don't panic. Me 'ands are all cut but it's nuffing – just blood. But I need some 'elp. Get some towels, anything!

(BUDDY *runs to the cupboard and gets towels.*)

BUDDY: I've got them.
TERRY: Okay, you can come in but don't be silly, right?
BUDDY: Okay?

(BUDDY *opens the door.* TERRY *is kneeling on the floor with his hands hanging down in the bath. His jacket is on the floor. There are drops of blood on the lino.*)

BUDDY: What happened?
TERRY: I've got to wash me 'ands. The disinfectant, get the disinfectant. Swill the sink down. I can't do it on me own. It's gotta be clean. Right, fill it wiv water put some disinfectant in. Right, now, 'elp me roll the sleeves of me shirt up.

(BUDDY *does everything as told.* TERRY *gets to his feet and sways over to the sink.*)

TERRY: Hang on to me, will you? Now don't let go. It's gonna 'urt like mad and I don't wanna fall and bang me nut.

(BUDDY *moves up behind* TERRY *and puts his arms round him. He hangs on, his head tight against* TERRY's *back.* TERRY *hesitates, then plunges his hands in with a gasp. His whole body stiffens with pain.* BUDDY *hangs on and gradually his dad relaxes.*)

TERRY: Blimey, it don't 'alf hurt. Okay – you can let go now.

BUDDY: Shall I call the doctor?

TERRY: No.

BUDDY: What happened?

TERRY: I came off me bike, didn't I. Get them towels. Wrap 'em round me 'ands.

(BUDDY *gets a towel ready.* TERRY *lifts one hand out of the water and wraps a towel round it.*)

TERRY: Right – tighter, tighter. Look mate, I've got to lie down – bring some more towels.

(BUDDY *follows his dad with towels.* TERRY *sways against the corridor wall and* BUDDY *supports him. They stagger to the bedroom.* TERRY *crashes down on the bed, face up.* BUDDY *lays towels under his hands.*)

TERRY: It's no good. It's coming through. Tighter. That's it. That's better. Listen, Buddy – if anyone asks, I was 'ere all night, right!

(BUDDY *nods.*)

BUDDY: I'll go and clear up.

(BUDDY *goes back to the bathroom, takes a towel and begins to wipe the blood off the floor. He notices a briefcase behind the door. He picks it up, wipes the blood then tries the catch. It is locked. He shakes it. It rattles.*)

TERRY: Give it here.

(TERRY *is in the doorway.* BUDDY *drops the case.*)

BUDDY: What is it?

TERRY: Nuffing.

BUDDY: Okay, then – I'll dump it outside.

TERRY: All right – it's jewellery if you must know, and it don't need you knocking it about.

BUDDY: Where did you get it?

TERRY: From a man.

BUDDY: You stole it, didn't you?

TERRY: No, I did not. I told you – I'm buying and selling antiques.

BUDDY: How did you cut yourself?

TERRY: I fell off me bike. Right?

BUDDY: Like hell, you did. You're a thief.

TERRY: Shut up and go to bed. Go on.

(BUDDY *is going to disobey but* TERRY *suddenly sways and looks desperate.* BUDDY *walks past him and goes to his bedroom. He throws himself down on the bed. A couple of seconds later* TERRY *shuffles past the open door into his own room. There is a groan as he lies down.* BUDDY *pulls the sleeping bag over his head.*)

SCENE 5 *The Clarks' kitchen. Day.*

(TERRY *is standing looking at the coffee powder he has spilt all over the draining board. He tries to pick up the jar but the towels wrapped round his hands make him clumsy and he drops it again.* BUDDY *comes in. They look at each other and* BUDDY *takes over as* TERRY *sits at the table.* BUDDY *puts some coffee in the mug, pours water on it, adds milk and sugar and gives it to* TERRY. TERRY *can't lift it and* BUDDY *holds it to his lips for him.*)

TERRY: Like a bloomin' baby. You'll 'ave to change me nappies next.

(BUDDY *does not respond to this attempt at humour.*)

BUDDY: You've got to stop it.

TERRY: What?

BUDDY: Stealing.
TERRY: I told you –
BUDDY: I don't care what you told me. I know.
TERRY: You don't know nuffin'.
BUDDY: Anything! Anything! You can't even talk properly.

(TERRY *slams out of his chair and goes towards the door.*)

BUDDY: You don't care about me. You'll go to prison, then what?
TERRY: Then you won't 'ave to put up wiv me, will yer?

SCENE 6 *The Clarks' living room.*

(TERRY *is sitting on the sofa – he has half unwrapped one of the towels.* BUDDY *comes in.*)

BUDDY: You ought to go to hospital.
TERRY: I don't need none of your advice. I want you to call someone for me.
BUDDY: What for?
TERRY: I can't do it meself, can I? I want someone to come and get that case, if you must know. It's too dangerous to keep 'ere.
BUDDY: It's stolen, isn't it?
TERRY: Yeah, all right – it's stolen. Satisfied?

(BUDDY *breaks. He slides down the wall in despair and huddles up crying.* TERRY *comes over and crouches down.*)

TERRY: Don't do that, Buddy. Come on.

(BUDDY *cannot stop.* TERRY *gets up and goes back to the sofa.*)

TERRY: Crying don't 'elp. Just makes it worse.
BUDDY: Can't be worse.
TERRY: Wanna bet? Being caught's worse.
BUDDY: Don't do it then.
TERRY: It ain't that easy.
BUDDY: Course it is. I stopped nicking from shops.
TERRY: I should 'ope you did. (*Sees the humour*) Blimey, what a pair.

BUDDY: I stopped. You can.
TERRY: This ain't nicking from shops. I'm in too deep.

(TERRY *lies back in despair now that he has said it.*)

BUDDY: I'll ring if you like.
TERRY: Ta. The number's 60065. Ask for Mr King.
BUDDY: Mr King?
TERRY: What's up?
BUDDY: Nothing.
TERRY: Tell 'im somefing went wrong and I want to see 'im 'ere. Tell 'im it's urgent. And when you're out see if you can get some bandages. I think that chemist shop's open on a Sunday.

(BUDDY *gets up, wiping his face. He goes to the door.*)

TERRY: Buddy. I'll try – all right?

SCENE 7 *Street.*

(BUDDY *is in a telephone box. We see him talking. He puts down the phone, comes out of the box and goes into the corner general shop.*)

SCENE 8 *The Clarks' living room.*

(BUDDY *is on his knees in front of the sofa finishing bandaging his dad's hands.* TERRY *is in pain and blood is already seeping through the bandage but he smiles as* BUDDY *finishes.*)

TERRY: Ace. Put some music on.

(BUDDY *gets up and is just moving to the records when the doorbell rings.*)

TERRY: That's him.

(BUDDY *goes to the front door and opens it.* DES KING *is standing there. He beams and taps* BUDDY *on the cheek.*)

MR KING: Terry's boy. Tubby, isn't it?
BUDDY: Buddy.

MR KING: That's right. Your dad in?

(*They go to the living room.*)

MR KING: Terry. Just been talking with your lad. What you done to his hair?

TERRY: Ain't me. They all got it round 'ere. Skin'eads or somefing. 'Orrible, ain't it?

MR KING: Looks a right villain. How old is he?

TERRY: Twelve.

BUDDY: I'm fourteen next week. And I'm not a skinhead.

MR KING: I expect he's got some homework to do, ain't you?

TERRY: Oh yeah. He's a right brain-box at school. Upstairs, Buddy.

(BUDDY *goes out – not quite closing the door. He makes a lot of stamping noise on the stairs then slowly tiptoes down to the door. We hear some of the following conversation from outside, then go inside.*)

MR KING: I told you not to use that number.

TERRY: I had to. I had trouble last night. It weren't my fault. I done me hands in on a wall. They're cut to pieces.

MR KING: I don't care what happened. I set up 56 as a safe house and I expect you to get the stuff there. I'm not pleased, Terry.

TERRY: I was thinking about leaving it off for a bit.

MR KING: A day or two till your hands are better. I've set up a couple of things for the weekend.

TERRY: Des, I've had enough.

MR KING: Now look, Terry – you owe me. Don't forget it. I've got things running nice. This is not some of your small time stuff. I've got customers in Europe and the States, and they expect delivery.

TERRY: Des.

MR KING: Don't you 'Des' me. A day or two for your hands but I want to see you at Croxley Street at eight on Friday evening. Understood? Good. I'll leave this there till then.

(BUDDY *tiptoes up the stairs and leans against the bedroom door, thinking. After a few moments there is the sound of the door opening below. He peeps down the stairs as* MR KING *comes out carrying the case.*)

MR KING: Well, I must love you and leave you. No, you sit there, Terry, and rest. I can find my own way out.

(BUDDY *dodges back. There is the sound of the front door opening and closing.* BUDDY *runs into his dad's bedroom and looks out of the window. He sees* MR KING *getting into a Jaguar. The car drives away.* BUDDY *turns, deep in thought.*)

SCENE 9 *The Clarks' living room.*

(TERRY *is lying on the sofa, defeated.* BUDDY *comes in and sits on the end of the sofa.*)

BUDDY: Well?

(TERRY *grunts.* BUDDY *tries to be casual.*)

BUDDY: Would he split on you?
TERRY: What do you mean?
BUDDY: I mean supposing the cops happened to pick him up with that bag?
TERRY: He's too sharp. Don't you worry about him.
BUDDY: Yeah, but supposing they did. Would he split?
TERRY: No. Des King might be a lot of things but 'e ain't a grass.

(*We move in to a big close-up of* BUDDY*'s face.*)

SCENE 10 *School corridor. Day.*

(*Members of 3E, including* BUDDY, CHARMIAN *and* JULIUS, *are walking along the corridor.* BUDDY *manages to draw* CHARMIAN *aside and stop.*)

BUDDY: Char, I've got to talk to you without Julius around. It's really important.

CHARMIAN: Okay. Where?
BUDDY: Meet me at the bike sheds after school.

SCENE 11 *Bike shed. Late afternoon.*

(It is raining and it is gloomy inside the shed. BUDDY *is squatting in the corner.* CHARMIAN *is standing with her back against the wall.)*

BUDDY: He tried. He said he wanted to stop but that fat pig won't let him.
CHARMIAN: What are you going to do?
BUDDY: I'm going to shop him.
CHARMIAN: Who?
BUDDY: Mr King.
CHARMIAN: How?
BUDDY: I've got a plan. But I need your help. Char, you've got to help me – please. If I don't do it my dad'll get caught, I know he will.
CHARMIAN: What do you want me to do?
BUDDY: Get Mrs Solomon to phone the police on Friday evening at eight and tell them she's seen someone breaking into 56.
CHARMIAN: I can't.
BUDDY: You've got to, please. It's the only way.
CHARMIAN: What'll happen?
BUDDY: The police'll come and find King there with all the stuff.
CHARMIAN: Buddy, he'll go to prison.
BUDDY: If he doesn't, my dad will.
CHARMIAN: Why Mrs Solomon? Why don't you ring?
BUDDY: It's got to be an adult or else the cops might not believe it. She doesn't have to say who she is. Just tell them she's seen something, then put the phone down. She'll do it – look how scared she is of what's going on there.
CHARMIAN: But your dad'll be there, too.
BUDDY: I'll keep him away. They'll just get Mr King.
CHARMIAN: How are you going to make sure your dad's not there?
BUDDY: I'm going to see my mum tomorrow.

(CHARMIAN *walks away across the deserted playground.* BUDDY *runs after her, calling.*)

BUDDY: Char.

(*She stops.*)

CHARMIAN: But I'm not doing it for Mrs Solomon or your dad. I'm doing it for you.

BUDDY: Thanks.

SCENE 12 *Street. Evening.*

(CAROL *and her friend,* JOYCE, *come down the road and turn into their house. They go down the basement steps.* BUDDY *steps out of the shadows. They start with fright.*)

CAROL: Buddy.

BUDDY: You said I could come and see you.

CAROL: Fine. Yeah. You'd better come in, then.

SCENE 13 *Carol's kitchen. Night.*

(CAROL, JOYCE *and* BUDDY *are sitting at the table.* CAROL *is showing photos.* BUDDY *looks at one without interest and passes it on to* JOYCE. CAROL *laughs at the one she has.*)

CAROL: Oh look, it's me and Buddy on the beach. Look at my hair! And look at you, Buddy – you were a right little fatty when you were a baby.

(*She passes the photo to* BUDDY *who looks at it with little interest and passes it to* JOYCE.)

JOYCE: Oh Carol, you look so young. Too young to have a baby almost.

CAROL: I was. Look at my hair, though.

JOYCE: It was all the style.

(BUDDY *glances at his watch.*)

BUDDY: I'll have to go in a minute.

(JOYCE *takes the hint.*)

JOYCE: Well, I've got to go right now – have a bath.

(*She gets up and goes out of the room.*)

CAROL: See you later. What do you think of Joyce? She's been fantastic to me – letting me share this place and everything. We just talk all the time about everything. She's like a sister.

(CAROL *reaches for a cigarette and stops.*)

CAROL: No. I'm trying to give them up. Talk about hard. I hope you haven't started. Does your dad still smoke his roll-ups?
BUDDY: Will you come and see him on Friday?
CAROL: Buddy. I can't.
BUDDY: Are you doing something?
CAROL: No.
BUDDY: Well? He loves you – I know.
CAROL: I just can't.
BUDDY: You said you missed us.
CAROL: I do. Supposing it didn't work out? I don't want to do all this to you all over again. I'm a bad enough mum as it is.
BUDDY: You keep saying that, and it's not true. Please, Mum. I don't mean come back for good. Just talk, that's all. Please. Dad'll be home on Friday if you come at half past seven. Please.
CAROL: All right. But it doesn't mean anything else.
BUDDY: No, just talk – that's all. Half past seven. Friday. Promise.
CAROL: Okay. Promise.

SCENE 14 *Buddy's bedroom.*

(BUDDY *is writing on a piece of paper his plan for Friday evening.*)

BUDDY: 7.30, phone Mrs Solomon. 8 o'clock, Mrs Solomon rings the police 8.10, the police arrive.

(BUDDY *writes 'King', then puts a big cross through the name.*)

SCENE 15 *Street. Night.*

(BUDDY *is waiting near a bus stop. He checks his watch and glances anxiously up the road. At last the bus is coming. It draws up and* CAROL *gets off.*)

CAROL: Well, here I am. Don't know why.
BUDDY: You look nice.
CAROL: That's something, I suppose.

(*They start to walk.*)

SCENE 16 *Buddy's street.*

(BUDDY *and* CAROL *come along the streets towards the house.* CAROL *turns into the garden, then stops as* BUDDY *does not follow her.*)

CAROL: Aren't you coming?
BUDDY: I thought it would be better ...
CAROL: Oh, great.

(*She turns and walks to the house.* BUDDY *waits until she rings the bell, and then belts away down the street.*)

SCENE 17 *A telephone box.*

(BUDDY *is dialling a number. He is ringing* MRS SOLOMON*'s house. The telephone rings in* MRS SOLOMON*'s room.* CHARMIAN *picks it up.*)

CHARMIAN: Buddy?
BUDDY: Yes. It's okay – my mum's there. They'll be at least an hour.
CHARMIAN: Buddy. Mr King's here. He got here about twenty past seven. He's in the house.
BUDDY: That's even better. (*He checks his watch*) Now, wait about two minutes, then get Mrs Solomon to ring. All she's got to say is that she's just seen someone break into 56, then put the phone down. I reckon the cops'll take about ten minutes. I'll be there by then if I run all the way.

CHARMIAN: Okay.
BUDDY: Right, I'm on my way.

(*He puts the phone down and begins to run down the street.*)

SCENE 18 *Mrs Solomon's room.*

(MRS SOLOMON *is sitting by the phone.* CHARMIAN *is looking at her watch.*)

CHARMIAN: Okay.

(MRS SOLOMON *picks up the phone and dials 999.*)

SCENE 19 *A street.*

(BUDDY *is running along the street. He stops at a main road where the traffic is so heavy that he cannot cross. He looks at his watch. Finally he darts across. Further along the street he slows to a fast walk so that he can catch his breath. He looks at his watch and begins to run again. Further on still,* BUDDY *is panting towards the main road opposite Croxley Street. He is just about to cross when he sees* MR KING *come down Croxley Street and go into the pub on the corner.* BUDDY *dodges out of sight.*)

BUDDY: No.

(*He checks his watch as* MR KING *goes into the pub, then dashes across the road and up Croxley Street.*)

SCENE 20 *54 Croxley Street.*

(BUDDY *runs into the garden, up the steps and bangs on the door.* CHARMIAN *opens the door. She steps aside to let him in and we see* MRS SOLOMON *in her wheelchair further down the hall.* BUDDY *does not go in. He cannot speak because he is so out of breath.*)

CHARMIAN: He's gone.
BUDDY: I know. He's gone to the pub. We've got to stop the cops.

CHARMIAN: We can't. They must be on their way. Just let them come. They won't know it was us.

BUDDY: He'll get away.

CHARMIAN: We can't help it.

(She listens. There is a distant roar.)

CHARMIAN: They're coming. Come inside, Buddy.

BUDDY: No.

(He runs down the steps as CHARMIAN *closes the door. He gets to the gate and peers round. Dazzling headlights shine in his eyes.)*

END OF EPISODE FOUR

EPISODE FIVE: EVERYDAY, IT'S A-GETTING CLOSER

SCENE 1 *Croxley Street.*

(*Dazzling headlights.* BUDDY *draws back, the noise fades and the headlights go out.* BUDDY *sees that it is a motorbike, and* TERRY *is getting off, removing his helmet.*)

BUDDY: Dad.
TERRY: What the 'ell are you doing 'ere?
BUDDY: Why aren't you with Mum?
TERRY: You 'ad no right to do that, Buddy.
BUDDY: What happened?
TERRY: What do you think 'appened?
BUDDY: Did she go?
TERRY: Course she went. You 'ad no right. What the 'ell are you doing 'ere?
BUDDY: I told the police. I told the police.

(TERRY *takes a second to register this, then quickly checks the street.*)

TERRY: When?
BUDDY: Ten minutes ago.

(TERRY *stares at him in confusion.*)

BUDDY: He made you do it. I wanted the cops to get him so you'd stop.

(TERRY *moves towards Number 56.* BUDDY *grabs him.*)

BUDDY: He's not there, he's gone. He's in the pub.
TERRY: Des King?

(BUDDY *nods.*)

TERRY: What about Ralph?
BUDDY: Who?
TERRY: Was there someone with Des? Tall. Simple-looking?
BUDDY: The Beast.

(TERRY *grabs* BUDDY *and shakes him.*)

TERRY: Was Ralph with him?

(BUDDY *shakes his head.* TERRY *lets him go and dashes into Number 56.*)

BUDDY: No, Dad.
TERRY: I can't leave Ralph. Go on. Get away.

(TERRY *rushes towards the house.* BUDDY *turns and looks down the street. He sees the blue revolving light of a police car in the distance. He dashes across the road and hides behind the pillar of a garden gate opposite. The police car glides to a halt. The light stops spinning. Two policemen get out quietly and head in towards Number 56.* BUDDY *slumps to the ground against the pillar. He holds his head in his hands in a state of misery. There are running footsteps. He looks up as* CHARMIAN *comes into the garden. She squats down beside him. He hunches back in despair.*)

CHARMIAN: Buddy.
BUDDY: Ralph. I didn't think about Ralph. Dad did.
CHARMIAN: Come over to Mrs Solomon's.

(*There is the sound of footsteps. They peer out.* DES KING *is coming along the road. He gets near Number 56, sees the police car, stops, then takes a few steps backwards. He turns and walks away quickly.* BUDDY *looks at* CHARMIAN *and sinks down again. A few moments later,* CHARMIAN *touches* BUDDY'*s arm. They peer round the gate again as* TERRY, THE BEAST *and the two policemen come out of 56. One of the policemen is carrying the incriminating briefcase.*

TERRY *and* THE BEAST *get into the back of the car. The policeman closes the door. The light is still on.* THE BEAST *puts his head forward on to his hands as if he is crying.* TERRY *puts his arm round* THE BEAST*'s shoulders to comfort him. The policemen get into the car and the car drives off. As soon as it has gone,* BUDDY *gets up and goes across the street to* TERRY*'s bike. He strokes the handlebars. He is lost.* CHARMIAN *comes up to him.*)

CHARMIAN: You'd better come home with me, Buddy.

(CHARMIAN *takes him by the arm and leads him away.*)

SCENE 2 *The Rybeeros' spare room. Night.*

(BUDDY *is lying on the bed with the light on. He is staring at the ceiling.* MRS RYBEERO *comes in. She is holding a pair of pyjamas.*)

MRS RYBEERO: Buddy. Here's a spare pair of pyjamas if you want. They're clean.

(BUDDY *does not respond.* MRS RYBEERO *puts them at the end of the bed and sits down beside them.*)

MRS RYBEERO: Ah know what you feeling, child – but don't you go blaming you daddy, now.

(BUDDY *looks at her for the first time.*)

MRS RYBEERO: It easy to do wrong – we all do it some times. That why Jesus say 'He who without sin, let him cast the first stone'. Remember that now.

(BUDDY *looks away.* MRS RYBEERO *goes to the door.*)

MRS RYBEERO: You can stay here long as you like.

(BUDDY *does not answer. She goes out and closes the door.*)

SCENE 3 *The Rybeeros' spare room. Morning.*

(CHARMIAN *knocks on the door.*)

CHARMIAN: Buddy – breakfast.

(*She opens the door and turns on the light.* BUDDY *is lying on the bed, his hands behind his head and his eyes open.*)

CHARMIAN: Are you okay?
BUDDY: I've got to go.
CHARMIAN: You don't have to.
BUDDY: The police'll look for me. They'll come here and ask. They'll put me in a home.
CHARMIAN: What about your mum?
BUDDY: After what I did?

(*He turns aside.*)

CHARMIAN: Buddy, don't cry.
BUDDY: I'm not (*He turns back – he's not*) I'm not going in a home.
CHARMIAN: Will you go back to your place?
BUDDY: They'll look there. I'm going somewhere – the last place they'll think of looking.
CHARMIAN: Where?
BUDDY: If you don't know, you don't have to lie. I'll stay there a bit and then go to the country. I can hide.
CHARMIAN: You can't live like that.
BUDDY: I won't go in a home. Swear you won't say anything.
CHARMIAN: Okay. I swear.

(BUDDY *turns away.* CHARMIAN *goes out, switching off the light.*)

SCENE 4 *Croxley Street. Day.*

(BUDDY *comes along the street. He is carrying a large bag. He checks – all clear – and makes it carefully to the side of Number 56. He looks up at* MRS SOLOMON'*s window, then goes down the side of the house to the back. He checks the back door – locked. But the same little window is open. He drags a dustbin under it, opens the window wide, chucks his stuff in and climbs up.*

SCENE 5 *Inside 56 Croxley Street. Night.*

(BUDDY *comes out of the kitchen door. Silence. He goes towards* THE BEAST*'s room.)*

TERRY (*voice over*): I heard a story tonight that'd give you the shivers. About this house in Croxley Street.

(BUDDY *puts down his stuff and moves to the stairs.*)

TERRY (*voice over*): Number 56.

(BUDDY *looks up the stairs.)*

BUDDY: Hello?

(*Nothing. He goes back towards the kitchen.*)

TERRY (*voice over*): Some geezer cut his wife's throat then he went and strung himself up.

(*Time has passed. In the semi-gloom – the boards over the window let in a little light –* BUDDY *is tidying up. He takes the* THE BEAST*'s bedclothes off and dumps them in the corner. He sees his dad's motorbike helmet and picks it up.*)

TERRY (*voice over*): Won't get rid of me as easy as that, mate. Oh, come on – don't let's row.

(BUDDY *moves to the bed and sits down.*)

TERRY (*voice over*): I know I don't talk posh.

(*'Gone', by Buddy Holly, starts to play as* BUDDY *puts down the helmet.*)

CAROL (*voice over*): Not a very good mum.

BUDDY (*voice over*): You are? Don't say that. You are.

(BUDDY *takes a photograph of his mum and dad out of his bag and leans it against the helmet. He looks at it.*)

CAROL (*voice over*): Buddy, you mustn't hate me for what I've done.

BUDDY (*voice over*): I don't. I love you.

SCENE 6 *Upstairs room in 56 Croxley Street.*

('Gone' continues to play as BUDDY *is looking at a print on the wall. He reads out the title.)*

BUDDY: 'Mother's Treasures.'

(He turns as he catches his reflection in a large mirror.)

CAROL *(voice over)*: Like father, like son.

SCENE 7 THE BEAST's *room again.*

*(*BUDDY *is lying on the bed in the sleeping bag. Candles are burning.)*

TERRY *(voice over)*: When you're dead, you're dead. Goodnight, mate.

(There is a creak. BUDDY *listens, scared. A draught blows the candles – shadows flicker on the ceiling. There's another creak.* BUDDY *listens then gets right down inside the sleeping bag.)*

SCENE 8 *Upstairs hallway in 56 Croxley Street.*

(The previous scene had no music but now 'Gone' begins again. BUDDY *is leaning against the doorway looking into one of the rooms, looking at the print. He turns, and walks across the hall. He stops and looks at the fragments of bottle on the floor. He sits down on the bottom stair and puts his head in his hands.)*

SCENE 9 *56 Croxley Street.*

(We zoom in to BUDDY *looking out of the attic window.)*

SCENE 10 *The phone room in 56 Croxley Street.*

*(*BUDDY *is sitting on the floor, dialling a number on the phone. 'Gone' stops playing. He has phoned the Speaking Clock. He listens, lying on the floor, as the man's voice begins to give the time.)*

BUDDY: Hello. It's my birthday. I'm fourteen.

SCENE 11 *Kitchen in 56 Croxley Street. Night.*

(BUDDY, *surrounded by candles, is lying awake on the bed. There is a noise. He listens. There is another noise. The door swings open.* BUDDY *closes his eyes, the door closes. He opens his eyes. We get a shot from his angle of* THE BEAST *looking down at him.* BUDDY *sits up.* RALPH *does not seem surprised. He walks over to where his things are piled, then turns.*)

BEAST: Where are the black boys?
BUDDY: They're not here. I'm by myself. One of them was a girl.

(BUDDY *unzips the sleeping bag and gets out. He hasn't got his jeans on – they're on the bed.* THE BEAST *looks away discreetly as* BUDDY *puts them on.* BUDDY *zips them up, then stands not quite knowing what to do.*)

BUDDY: I'm sorry I'm in your house. – I haven't got anywhere else to go.
BEAST: It's my house. Uncle Des told me. 'It's your house, Ralphie – and that's that.'
BUDDY: I thought you ... weren't here. You went away with the police.
BEAST: I didn't do anything. Mr Clark told them I didn't steal anything. Mr Clark told them he did it.
BUDDY: Yeah.

(RALPH *looks round the room. He points to the stove.*)

BUDDY: I brought it. You can cook your food on it.

(RALPH *nods and smiles. He points to the cans.*)

BEAST: Beans.
BUDDY: Do you want some?

(RALPH *smiles and nods.*)

BUDDY: Okay. I brought paper plates, too.

SCENE 12 *Kitchen in 56 Croxley Street. Night.*

(BUDDY *and* RALPH *are sitting on the floor. They finish their beans and put down their plates.* RALPH *moves his so that it is beside* BUDDY's. *He looks up and smiles.* BUDDY *smiles back.* BUDDY *gets up and takes his sleeping bag off the bed and starts to roll it up. He decides.*)

BUDDY: Ralph, would you mind if I stayed?

(RALPH *stands up and considers.*)

BEAST: You can stay.

(*He picks up his bedclothes and puts them roughly on his bed. He sits down.* BUDDY *takes his cue and puts his things against the wall and sits down.* RALPH *smiles. He's happy.*)

BUDDY: Is your Uncle Des's name Mr King?
BEAST: Des King. He's nice to me. He said I didn't have to stay in Chandos House. I didn't like it there. It's for loonies.

(*They both watch as one of the candles gutters and goes out.* BUDDY *gets another one and lights it. He puts it in the bottle.*)

BEAST: Haven't you got a mum and dad?

(BUDDY *does not answer. He finishes sticking the candle in the bottle and goes back to his sleeping bag.*)

BEAST: I haven't got a mum and dad. I haven't got ...
BUDDY: You've got Uncle Des ...

(RALPH *nods but he is still troubled.*)

BEAST: Uncle Des was my ... Uncle Des was my m–my mum's brother. My mum. My – dad – killed – her.
BUDDY: Your dad ...
BEAST: He hanged. My dad hanged himself. He did it. When I got home from school. I found them.

(*We get a huge close-up of* RALPH, *eyes fixed open. Gradually we move back. His eyes blink again. We get a close-up of* BUDDY. *He watches as* RALPH *lies down and covers himself up slowly.*)

BEAST: I don't like the dark.
BUDDY: Nor do I. I'll keep the candles going.

(RALPH *suddenly sits up.*)

BEAST: Have you got a mum and dad?

(BUDDY *nods.*)

BEAST: You're lucky.
BUDDY: I know.

SCENE 13 *Kitchen in 56 Croxley Street. Day.*

(*Light is coming through the window. A couple of candles burn low next to the sleeping* RALPH. BUDDY *is cramming his sleeping bag into his bag, then thinks about the gas stove. He decides to leave it for* RALPH. *He tiptoes over to* RALPH, *and shakes him lightly.* RALPH *wakes but is very sleepy.*)

BUDDY: Ralph. Can you hear me? It's morning. I've got to go now. But I'll come back and see you soon. Okay?

(RALPH *nods.* BUDDY *blows out the candles.*)

BUDDY: It's day now. Thanks.

(*He gets up and goes out of the door.*)

SCENE 14 *Carol's flat. Day.*

(BUDDY *is ringing the bell of the flat.* JOYCE *opens the door. She's in her dressing gown and is sleepy.*)

BUDDY: Is my mum in?
JOYCE: Where've you been? Everybody's been looking for you.
BUDDY: Where's my mum?
JOYCE: She's not here.

BUDDY: Where is she?

JOYCE: Round your house. She's been going crazy – thanks to you. They both have.

BUDDY: They? My dad's there?

JOYCE: Yes.

BUDDY: How?

JOYCE: He's out on bail. Your mum put up bail. Buddy! Buddy!

(*But he does not stop. He's off up the steps and away.*)

SCENE 15 *Street. Day.*

(*We see* BUDDY *racing along, dodging through crowds.*)

SCENE 16 *Outside Buddy's house. Day.*

(BUDDY *comes running along the street and up to the front door. He rings and rings, panting with exhaustion. The door opens – it is* CAROL.)

CAROL: Buddy.

(*They wrap their arms round each other. After a moment we see, over* BUDDY'*s shoulder,* TERRY *coming out of the living room.* BUDDY *sees him and* CAROL *and he slowly breaks their embrace.* CAROL *steps aside.* BUDDY *takes a step inside.*)

BUDDY: Dad.

TERRY: You do two things, Buddy Clark: cry or say you're sorry, and you're out that door. Right?

(BUDDY *struggles not to cry but as his face screws up,* TERRY *cuts in.*)

TERRY: I didn't 'ear you say 'Yes'.

BUDDY: Yes.

TERRY: Right. And there's another fing before your mum starts in about where you bin. It might be six months before me trial comes up in court and I've promised 'er I'll get a job. You said them black friends – they still looking for drivers?

(BUDDY *runs to* TERRY *and crushes himself against his chest.* CAROL *closes the front door.*)

SCENE 17 *The Clarks' living room. Six months later.*

(*Music: 'Heart Beat', Buddy Holly.* BUDDY, *his hair grown again, is leaning against the window sill with a book of notes in his hand. He is skipping through looking for questions. Every so often he glances out of the window.* CAROL *is sitting in a chair.*)

CAROL: What's the time?

BUDDY: Half eight. You asked ten minutes ago. Right, next question: name five types of retail outlet.

CAROL: Chain stores. Department Stores. Corner shops. Um. Oh, I'm useless at this. I'll never pass.

BUDDY: Yes, you will. You got them all yesterday. You're not concentrating. Markets.

CAROL: Supermarkets. Hypermarkets.

BUDDY: There you are. Next name four methods of obtaining credit.

CAROL: Credit card. Mortgage ...

BUDDY: He's here.

(BUDDY *dumps the notes and runs to the door.*)

SCENE 18 *Outside the Clarks' house. Evening.*

(TERRY *and* MR RYBEERO *are getting out of a* RYBEERO's *taxi as* BUDDY *comes out of the door and on to the pavement.*)

TERRY: Well, Malcolm. (*He pats the top of the car*) Won't be needing this tomorrow.

MR RYBEERO: Hello, Buddy.

TERRY: Wotcher, mate.

MR RYBEERO: Listen, Terry – good luck. Whatever happen – there always be a job for you with us.

TERRY: See you, Malcolm. See you.

(*He shakes* MR RYBEERO*'s hand. Then* TERRY *puts his arm round* BUDDY *and they walk towards the house. The taxi drives off.*)

TERRY: Last one in's a wally.

(*They dart towards the house.*)

SCENE 19 *Buddy's bedroom. Night.*

(BUDDY *is in bed. The light is off but the door is open. He is listening as* CAROL *and* TERRY *come up the stairs.* CAROL *passes the door but* TERRY *comes in.*)

TERRY: You asleep?
BUDDY: No.

(TERRY *sits on the bed.*)

TERRY: I'm gonna plead guilty tomorrow. Never know – might get a bit less like that. Maybe a year, maybe less.

(BUDDY *rolls over to hide his face.*)

TERRY: 'Ere, you keep 'elping your mum wiv 'er exams.

(BUDDY *nods and* TERRY *ruffles his hair.*)

TERRY: Two flipping geniuses in the family – that's all I need. Look after 'er, won't you, though, eh? And you.

(BUDDY *nods.* TERRY *gets up and goes to the door.* BUDDY *turns to look at him.* TERRY *winks.*)

TERRY: It'll soon go.

(*He goes out, closing the door.*)

SCENE 20 *The Clarks' kitchen.*

(CAROL *is slumped at the table, head forward on her hands. Her handbag is next to her head. She hasn't taken off her smart overcoat.*

She has been dressed for the trial. She lifts her head and looks at BUDDY.)

CAROL: Eighteen months. They gave him eighteen months.

(*She lies face down again, one hand over her shoulder.* BUDDY *takes it.*)

CAROL: They let me see him for a bit. He reckons he'll have to do fifteen. He was joking around. You know him.

(BUDDY *continues to hold her hand. She finally sits up and rubs her eyes.*)

CAROL: You know what he said? He said he wanted us to make a cup of tea and play a Buddy Holly song. He wrote it down for you.

(*She fumbles in her bag and finds the piece of paper. She gives it to* BUDDY.)

CAROL: I'll make the tea.

(*In the living room,* BUDDY *kneels on the floor surrounded by records. He finds the one he wants and takes it out of its cover. He lays it on the record deck as* CAROL *comes in with two cups of tea. She sits down as* BUDDY *starts the machine. It is Buddy Holly singing 'Everyday'. As he reaches the last line of the first verse,* BUDDY *turns round to look at his mum.*)

THE END

Some suggested responses

Episode one

First impressions

1 Look closely at Scene 3 and answer the following questions:
(a) What are Terry and Carol rowing about?
(b) What evidence is there to suggest that these rows happen quite often? (Do the first two brief visual scenes add to the intended impression here?)
(c) How is Buddy coping with the atmosphere in his family?

2 Does Buddy feel 'under pressure' at school? How?

3 'Like father, like son' becomes an important line which is repeated throughout the five episodes. How are Buddy and Terry alike?

4 In the novel, Buddy thinks 'There must be something wrong with me'. What does he think is 'wrong' with him?

5 Can you explain Buddy's interest in death and dying?

6 Describe the tensions felt by Buddy *before* Carol's departure and how these tensions develop after she has left.

The dramatisation and the novel

Chapter One of the novel and the events it describes are expanded upon in the first episode of the dramatisation. Look at both, identify the differences and say which you prefer. (Do the changes alter the emphasis significantly? Are the changes indications of any important differences between a play and a novel?)

An alternative view

The following suggestions invite you to look at some of the events of the first episode from a different perspective. Choose one for a piece of writing of your own.

1 Write a scene in which Carol, having left Buddy and Terry, arrives at her friend's flat. (The friend's name is Joyce.) She

explains what has happened, why she has left home and asks Joyce whether she can stay.

2 Mr Normington talks to a colleague in the staffroom about Buddy, complaining that Buddy is not the 'right type' for 3E. The other teacher defends Buddy.

3 A letter from Terry to Carol. What would he say?

Your own writing

1 You arrive home from school in the usual way. Your parents are not there (or do not arrive home from work at their usual time). What happens? How do you feel? What do you do? It would be interesting to contrive a situation which involves your being left alone in the house for the whole night. Your parents could perhaps return the next day. Where have they been? Are you (and your behaviour and attitudes) the cause of their night away?

2 Write a description of an empty old house. Does it have 'a past'?

Episode two

Terry and Buddy

1 What difference does the money make to Buddy? How does it help? How does it worry Buddy? Is it enough?

2 What do the Rybeeros have in their family which Buddy notices is missing from his own? How does he try to bring those qualities into his own home?

3 Find examples to illustrate these two statements:
(a) Buddy likes the fact that Terry is different from most dads and enjoys being with him.
(b) Terry embarrasses Buddy and irritates him.

4 Look closely at Scene 12 and answer the following questions:
(a) What do Terry's attitudes to the shop he used to own and to the Rybeeros tell you about him?
(b) Although Terry mentions starting another shop, Buddy

still suggests that Terry might apply for a job as a taxi driver. Why?

(c) Why does Terry become angry?

(d) What do you think Buddy's feelings are at the end of the scene?

The Beast

1 Look again at the references to 56 Croxley Street in Episode One. How is 'The Beast' further developed in this episode into a figure to be feared?

2 Can you see any connection between the appearance of The Beast as a real character in the story and Buddy's inner fears about himself and his problems at home?

3 Can you identify the techniques which Nigel Hinton (the writer) uses to make The Beast's first appearance frightening?

Your own work

In groups, discuss your answer to the first question in this section (about money).

As a group, design your own questionnaire about 'money and young people'. Try to include factual questions (for example: How much pocket money do you get? How do you spend it?) *and* more complex questions about money and relationships.

Once the questionnaire is agreed upon, it can be given to another group for completion.

Tabulate (collect, list and summarise) the answers.

Were the right questions asked?

Are your conclusions revealing? (Are they what you expected or did they contain surprises?)

Episode three

In this episode there are two particularly powerful scenes – Terry at the Parents' Consultation, and Carol meeting Buddy in the café to explain her reasons for leaving. Look closely at the two scenes and answer in detail the following questions.

1 Buddy feels, at the beginning of both scenes, 'embarrassed and awkward'. What makes him feel this way?

2 Both scenes bring him closer to his parents. Can you explain how?

3 Would it be true to say that Buddy's view of his parents alters because of the events in this episode? If so, what is this alteration – or new understanding?

4 The episode begins with a scene in which Buddy meets The Beast face to face. In a stage direction the writer says of this encounter: 'The Beast's threatening appearance has dissolved'. Why has this happened? How does this moment set the tone for the whole episode?

Through other eyes

Choose an appropriate *form* to develop one of the following ideas (for example: a story, a scene, an interview, a letter, etc.).

1 The Beast: How does he sees the events so far? Does he understand? How does he speak? How does he see the world around him? What does he feel about people being frightened of him?

2 Mrs Rybeero: How does she see Buddy? What does she think of Terry? What does she think of the school? How does she see her own family's future?

3 Joyce: Although she is largely an 'off-stage' character, she must be fairly close to Carol and what is happening to her. How does she see the situation? What does she think (hope) will happen. What are the problems she has in having Carol staying with her?

Your own work

The Parents' Evening.

Tell your own story about your parents going to your school to talk about you. Describe the events leading up to their departure, how they react, speak and feel whilst they are there, and how they communicate all this to you when they return home. (How do you feel throughout all this?)

Episode four

'Grass' (1)

It is Buddy's intention to have Mr King arrested by the police. His plan aims to save his father, but there are obvious risks.

1 Construct an argument (in writing or discussion) which convinces Buddy that he is *right* to do what he plans.

2 Construct an argument which opposes Buddy's plans on the grounds that it is *wrong* to 'grass'.

3 Assuming that you agree (if not, why not?) that Terry ought to end his involvement with Des King, what would you advise Buddy to do in order to bring about his father's withdrawal from criminal activities (apart from telling the police, as he plans to do)?

'Grass' (2)

In groups, discuss this issue of 'grassing'. Is it ever right to 'grass'? Give examples. When is it wrong to tell on someone? Perhaps you might list when it is right and when it is wrong. Look at your lists and see if you can formulate 'rules' or 'guidelines' on this issue. Share and discuss your conclusions with the rest of your class.

Prediction

It looks as though Mr King is going to escape at the end of this episode. Discuss what you think is going to happen in the last episode. Will Terry be arrested? Will Carol return home? Will Buddy ever be able to face Terry again? From Buddy's point of view, what do you think would be the best outcome?

Your own writing

A close friend of yours is involved in something which you very strongly believe is wrong (for example, shoplifting, truanting, drugs, stealing from other friends, etc.). Describe your attempts to stop him or her – in a story. Do you succeed? How?

Episode five

Outcomes

1 Terry sacrifices his chance of escape in order to save Ralph (The Beast). Is this something new in his character? Or was this quality there all the time?
2 Analyse (and list) Buddy's thoughts during his period alone in the house. Does your list include all the main concerns which Buddy has had during the five episodes?
3 How does the discovery that Ralph is the son of the couple who died in the house help Buddy to sort out what he ought to do?
4 Look at the scene in which Buddy arrives home. Do Carol and Terry react as you might have expected? Have they changed?

Looking at the whole story

A.
1 The figure of Buddy Holly and Terry's feelings towards him represent an important 'image' in the five episodes. Discuss the importance of this image and how it relates to Terry, Buddy, Carol and the way the plays develop.
2 How does the story of Ralph (The Beast) act as a powerful 'sub-plot' (that is, an element of the whole story which echoes and highlights aspects of the main story)?
3 Like all good pieces of writing, *Buddy* has many layers. It can be seen to be 'about' a number of issues – growing up, learning to think of others, marriage, unemployment, outsiders, loyalty and betrayal, prejudice, the relationship between parents and children, the problems of communication, and so on. You may be

able to add further 'themes' to this list. Which aspects of the story do *you* think are most important – in other words, which leave the greatest impression on you?

4 Look at the techniques used by Nigel Hinton in his narrative. Try to analyse the structure of each episode and see if you can come to any conclusions about telling a story in episodes. (How has he kept your interest? How has he developed the characters? How does he create suspense and atmosphere?)

5 If you have the opportunity, compare this dramatisation with the novel. Are there differences? Are there omissions in the plays – or additions? Is the emphasis changed in any way? Which do you find more effective and why?

B.

1 Ten years on: Buddy and Charmian Rybeero meet by chance – perhaps on a train. Buddy tells her what has happened to him and his family since Terry was released from prison – perhaps they moved away from the area on his release.

2 Write a newspaper article – 'Boy shops father' – telling the story, as a news report would, of the events leading to Terry's arrest and court appearance.

3 Ralph – tell the story of what becomes of Ralph.

4 Describe a character who (a) lives in the past, *or* (b) refuses to grow up.